Leadership: Project and Human Capital Management

Leadership: Project and Human Capital Management

John McManus

AMSTERDAM • BOSTON • HEIDELBERG • LONDON
NEW YORK • OXFORD • PARIS • SAN DIEGO
SAN FRANCISCO • SINGAPORE • SYDNEY • TOKYO

Butterworth-Heinemann is an imprint of Elsevier

Butterworth-Heinemann is an imprint of Elsevier
Linacre House, Jordan Hill, Oxford OX2 8DP
30 Corporate Drive, Suite 400, Burlington, MA 01803

First published 2006

British Library Cataloguing in Publication Data
A catalogue record for this book is available from the British Library

Library of Congress Cataloguing in Publication Data
A catalogue record for this book is available from the Library of Congress

ISBN 13: 978 0 7506 6896 5
ISBN 10: 0 7506 6896 2

For information on all Butterworth-Heinemann publications visit our web site at
http://books.elsevier.com

Printed and bound by CPI Group (UK) Ltd, Croydon, CR0 4YY

Transferred to Digital Print 2011

Contents

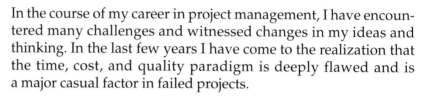

Introduction to the Book

In the course of my career in project management, I have encountered many challenges and witnessed changes in my ideas and thinking. In the last few years I have come to the realization that the time, cost, and quality paradigm is deeply flawed and is a major casual factor in failed projects.

A few years ago, I facilitated a series of business-related workshops for a major project I was involved in at that time. During and after these workshops my self-awareness and understanding of how other people viewed this paradigm increased significantly. What I experienced alarmed me as I began to comprehend the absolute ineffectiveness of this model and all its shortcomings. After that experience, my focus and thinking moved towards offering the business world and project community an alternative paradigm based on the model of *leadership, stakeholder, and risk management*.

Having spent 20 years of my career in project management and having delivered £100 million in earned value, I firmly believe that the project stakeholder community, and not the management are the key to delivering successful projects, and that the project manager that flourishes will be the one that empowers team members, and allows them the freedom to speak their minds about what needs to be done and to take risks without reprisals. I also believe that too many senior managers and their acolytes devalue what project managers do, many of these senior managers relish too much the paranoia and politicking that goes on within organizations.

This is the third book of mine that discusses what I believe to be contemporary issues within this project-management paradigm. My previous two books focussed on "stakeholder and risk management". This book *Leadership in Project Management* completes the circle.

In brief, this book is divided into seven chapters; Chapter 1 provides the impetus and conceptual background for the book as a whole. Chapter 2 describes the process of team building and reviews a range of principles, theories, and practical guidelines that can be used to build teams.

Chapter 3 covers some notions of decision making. In particular how leadership contributes to and influences the decision-making process. In Chapter 4, I discuss some aspects of power and how leadership manages conflict. It is argued that leadership involves more than taking ownership — it involves engaging others in the complete management process. In Chapter 5, I introduce the concept of stakeholder communication and discuss some of the ideas and issues associated with it.

In Chapter 6, I focus the debate on leadership ethics and governance and consider some of the political, economic, and social issues. As with most ethical debates legality and stewardship is considered to be a key and relevant issue for management. Our debate focuses on what leadership means in this context.

Finally, in Chapter 7, I introduce a number of reading materials and essay material to reinforce the key subject matter discussed in the previous six chapters.

In writing this book, I have attempted to draw on my practical experience and where appropriate those of other practitioners working in project management. The summary points at the end of each chapter serve as a review guide or may be used by the reader as a framework for discussion. Whilst I have attempted to refrain from duplication, some repetition within chapters is inevitable. I believe, however, that this helps the reader by strengthening the points made in previous chapters. I have used the terms "leader" and "project manager" wherever appropriate but also interchangeably throughout the book. In essence, however, they are deemed to be the same entity.

John McManus

Acknowledgements

I would like to acknowledge the help and assistance of a few people in the preparation of this book. The most prominent amongst these are Dr Chris Sauer, Larry Cowan, Bo Bennett, Professor Trevor Wood-Harper, Dr John Gottman, Dr Carter McNamara, Elaine Boyes, Paul Tarplett, Dr David Gould, Dr Stafan C Gueldenberg, Dr Werner Hoffmann, Dr Marshall Goldsmith, Howard Morgan, and Marie J. Kane.

I would also like to say a big thank you to my colleagues within the Department of Corporate Strategy at the University of Lincoln who provided some insight into the challenges of leadership.

I cannot conclude this list without acknowledging my friend and mentor Dr Jessie Laurence from my days at Crotonville and GE. I would also like to say a big thank you to my former "management team" that is: Stuart, Pero, Neville, Dan, Mark, Lee, John, Sally, Peter, Don, Jenny, and Neil. Some great times, lots of fun, and elements of genius; I count myself lucky to have been first among equals.

Rocks

As this man stood in front of the group of high-powered over-achievers he said, "Okay, time for a quiz." Then he pulled out a gallon, wide-mouthed Mason jar and set it on a table in front of him. He then produced about a dozen fist-sized rocks and carefully placed them, one at a time, into the jar. When the jar was filled to the top and no more rocks would fit inside, he asked, "Is this jar full?"

Everyone in the class said, "Yes."

Then he said, "Really?" He reached under the table and pulled out a bucket of gravel. Then he dumped some gravel in and shook the jar causing pieces of gravel to work themselves down into the spaces between the big rocks. Then he asked the group once more, "Is the jar full?"

By this time the class was onto him. "Probably not," one of them answered.

"Good!" he replied. He reached under the table and brought out a bucket of sand and started dumping the sand in until it went into all the spaces left between the rocks and the gravel. Once more he asked the question, "Is this jar full?"

"No!" the class shouted.

Once again he said, "Good!" He then grabbed a pitcher of water and began to pour it in until the jar was filled to the brim. Then he looked up at the class and asked, "What is the point of this illustration?"

One eager beaver raised his hand and said, "The point is, no matter how full your schedule is, if you try really hard, you can always fit some more things into it!"

"No," the speaker replied, "that's not the point. The truth this illustration teaches us is: If you don't put the big rocks in first, you'll never get them in at all."

What are the "big rocks" in your life? A project that you want to accomplish? Time with your loved ones? Your faith? Your education? Your finances? A cause? Teaching or mentoring others?

Remember to put these BIG ROCKS in first or you will never get them in at all.

(Author Unknown)

1 Leadership and Team Building

1.1 Why leadership in project management is crucial?

Projects are rarely the domain of any individual; but leadership in project management is the province of the project manager – or is it? Leadership will become the central driver of the 21st century economy, and the future state of project management is now tied to the leadership, stakeholder,[1] and risk[2] management paradigm. Success in the deployment of software projects is, in turn, tied to the dynamics and constraints of global markets, governmental forces, internal competencies, and stakeholder knowledge.

Those individuals engaged in the construction and delivery of software projects must have a clear and concise business vision if they want their projects to survive and thrive through turbulence. Project managers must have a clear understanding of what business they are in and this is absolutely critical when communicating project or team objectives (a point we will return to in Chapter 2). Teams must be developed to support the business vision and project objectives. It is useful to bear in mind that successful projects and bottom line results come through your project team and other stakeholders but leadership is a vital component. Leadership is about the mix of "vision and the ability" to guide people to ensure that they all try and meet the objective as a team. Research by Kouzes and Posner into leadership highlighted that leadership skills most frequently practised are enabling others to act and modelling the way, followed by

---

[1]A full treatise of this subject may be found in the author's book *Managing Stakeholders in Software Development Projects*, Elsevier, Butterworth-Heinemann (2005), ISBN 0750664554.
[2]A full treatise of this subject may be found in the author's book *Risk Management in Software Development Projects*, Elsevier, Butterworth-Heinemann (2004), ISBN 0750658673.

encouraging the heart and challenging the process. Inspiring a shared vision is the least frequently practised skill by managers (see Table 1.2).

The issue here is that any project manager who aspires to be an effective leader must not only lead own project team efforts, but must also be seen to do so by the client and wider business stakeholders. Increasingly, they must do this against a background of a progressively more complex and global business environment far removed from the structured problems area of software development and convince their stakeholders and colleagues that they truly understand the issues of managing projects in a fast-paced 21st century business.

Although the body of knowledge about project failure has deepened, too many project managers are still fire fighting and fighting rearguard actions, and as a consequence, project managers are under constant pressure to convince their paymasters that they add value to the organization. A recent survey conducted by IBM noted that only 13% of the organizations surveyed rated their ability to respond to changing business conditions, while less than 10% believed their companies are reactive to their top three business threats. A further 60% described the major barrier to change as limited internal skills, capabilities, and leadership. Most managers who participated in the survey felt that significant deficiencies in leadership skills, both inside and outside their organization, threaten the growth of their organizations. This point reinforces a vital message about leadership: you must be highly sensitive to the wider conditions in which your business operates. For example, by 2010 only 20% of the UK workforce will be white able-bodied male under 45 – consider the resource and cultural implications for firms and those managers responsible for delivering global projects; now, more than ever, organizations have to appraise the wider socioeconomics operating, and environmental factors under which their projects will be delivered.

In some respects, leadership is difficult to define in absolute terms. Leadership gurus Jim Kouzes and Barry Posner identified a number of key practices that revealed how leaders get extraordinary things done in their organizations. Kouzes and Posner wanted to know what people did when they were at their "personal best" in leading others. Their then-radical assumption was that, by asking ordinary people to describe extraordinary experiences, they would find patterns of success. Kouzes and Posner initially collected more than 2000 long and short surveys and conducted in-depth interviews with line supervisors, managers,

Table 1.1 Important characteristics of successful project managers

Characteristic	Rank
Commercial awareness	1
Confidence	2
Preparedness to take risks	3
Understanding of information technology	4
Integrity	5
Goal orientation	6
Written communication	7
Attention to detail	8
Planning	9
Problem solving	10
Enthusiasm	11
Preparedness to work in a team	12
Delegation	13
Prior success	14
Leadership	15
Energy	16
Stakeholder management	17
Conflict resolution	18
Time management	19
Securing resources	20
Ability to manage change	21
Oral communication	22
Initiative	23
Perspective	24
Understanding business processes	25

This table is reproduced with permission from the State of IT Project Management in the UK 2002–2003, Report by Chris Sauer and Christine Cuthbertson, Templeton College, University of Oxford, p. 2.

and chief executive officers. Since the publication of their book in 1987 they have gone on to collect many thousands of cases. In analysing these case studies, they have uncovered five practices of exemplary leadership – the common practices associated with personal bests (see Table 1.2). Their research indicates that organizations and their leaders who engage in these five practices achieve desirable results. They are more effective as leaders, more credible, more motivating, and they attain teamwork, commitment, productivity, and lower turnover.

Each of these practices will place different demands on project managers and those that are led by them, and few project managers are unusually successful in mastering all five practices. For example, in "modelling the way", project managers often rely on sharing information and intelligence when dealing

Table 1.2 Five practices of exemplary leadership (after Kouzes and Posner, 1987)

Practice	Interpretation
Modelling the way	Setting the example, living out one's professed values, and creating small wins
Challenge the process	Searching for and accepting challenging opportunities, and taking risks
Inspiring a shared vision	Holding and communicating a vision of what is possible, and getting everyone aligned to a common purpose
Enabling others to act	Fostering collaboration and building energetic, winning teams based on mutual trust, understanding, and shared goals
Encouraging the heart	Recognizing contributions and celebrating accomplishments

with peers, senior managers, and stakeholders within their respective organizations, and in many instances shared intelligence is based on quid pro quo (a form of transactional management (see Section 1.6) transactions, which may not always lead to win/win outcomes or foster mutual respect and trust (a point we return to in Chapter 4).

1.2 Challenges in leadership

Given the extent of management literature published in recent years, it might be thought that leadership in project management is no longer an issue. However, few writers actually define leadership and the context is generally not in project management. For the last 30 years, the challenges within project management and software development have focussed on maximizing the time, cost, and quality paradigm. Although leadership is a concern, sadly for many it comes lower down the list of key characteristics than understanding and keeping pace with information technology. Those responsible for initiating projects within organizations still look to the time, cost, and quality paradigm as a way of prioritizing projects and the work that needs undertaking to deliver them. In many respects, this paradigm reinforces the value of technical skills above the softer skills that many aspiring project managers need and makes it difficult for project managers (future leaders) to get out of the technology ghettos many find themselves in.

In the interests of maximizing the time, cost, and quality paradigm, the presumption is that those who are being led are motivated to follow rather than coerced to do so. Interestingly, the UK view on leadership is simply that whoever is at the head of the pack is a leader, regardless of whether the pack is motivated to follow voluntarily. Motivation rarely appears on the top 10 concerns' list of key decision makers. For example, a recent survey in 2004 (see Table 1.3) on the top 10 concerns of information technology directors placed managing budgets as the top priority and project management as their least priority, indicating that project management, even today, is very undervalued in many organizations. Motivating subordinates and team members did not make the list.

Motivation is important to the success of any project undertaking because it is essentially about winning the hearts and minds of people. It is also clear that what may be characterized as project "management" is equally important because this is about getting things done. Can the two be reconciled? For this, it is necessary to turn to a fundamental principle underpinning the concept of project management.

Information technology projects are usually initiated in the context of change; software development projects, however, tend to be different from normal – perhaps incremental change in that they have a clear set of objectives to be realized within the time, cost, and quality paradigm. Success depends on the application of a four-step sequence: first Plan, then Do (produce), Check (monitor), and Act (motivate). This is the basis of every project life cycle (McManus, 2001).

In the planning phase for example, the project manager conducts the project team and other main stakeholders through formal

Table 1.3 Top 10 concerns of IT directors

Rank	Concern
1	Managing budgets
2	Aligning IT with business
3	Keeping pace with technology
4	Recruiting training and managing staff
5	Dealing with senior management
6	Managing time and resources
7	Security
8	Dealing with technology
9	Dealing with customers
10	Project management

Source: *Managing Information Strategies*, April 2004, p. 42.

and informal decision making in order to reach agreed goals and objectives. This process involves a high degree of interaction and a formulation of organizational strategies. It takes time and is challenging. The development of the resulting requirements (both functional and nonfunctional) may require a number of iterations and reruns. This is especially true at the outset when it is important to flush out the customer's needs. Therefore, visioning, intelligence gathering, and developing a compelling reason and appropriate strategies are the all-important issues. These issues also form the essential basis for effective team development (a point we will return to in Chapter 2).

One of the prime challenges faced by project managers is that of getting people to accept responsibility for their own actions and take ownership of risk. Although software engineering attracts creative and bright individuals, many of them by nature tend to be risk averse and, human nature being what it is, many abdicate responsibility. Often project managers have to use a plethora of emotional, motivational, and reward strategies for different people – taken at face value this may be considered a useful approach to achieving objectives, however, it is time consuming and in many instances, counterproductive to team building. For example, while the emotional part of the team's motivation can be built up by the project manager, the material incentives can create a problem. If the project team members are from the same organization only, the incentive scheme should be clear and valid for everyone and there should be no difference either on the material or on the emotional level.

Project teams, however, are increasingly brought together from different organizations and cultures, and this tends to increase the emotional stress and pressures on the project manager to achieve the objectives of the project.While the project manager might eventually be able to develop the same mixture of emotional support and recognition for all team members, the material incentives may remain different, depending on the organization each participant belongs to. Differences in material rewards can introduce a lot of pressure in teams over time; typically the lower-rewarded team members get frustrated and lose some of their motivation. If people are joining your project team from different organizations, it is important that they should fit into your culture or you will have to make structural arrangements that compensate for differences.

To counter some of these issues many organizations link performance on projects to the wider social and economic benefits of the business. In the last 5 years flexible benefits have become the norm in many large systems integration companies for rewarding and retaining project personnel. Such schemes do not eradicate all the risk reward anomalies but they do help to distribute incentive benefits more equitably. For example, the following comment was made by Kathryn Dolan, HR Project Manager for Fujitsu on the introduction of Fujitsu online flexible benefits system.

> *Motivation has also improved with the implementation of the system, according to Dolan. Following significant periods of change over a number of years, there were major inconsistencies and legacy issues in the way employees were rewarded. Since adopting online flex with 4th Contact, there's been a positive shift in our perception as an employer. The inconsistencies have been eliminated and now people can see a transparent and equitable reward structure. There are many less pay-focused debates amongst employees.*

> *(Source: Fujitsu Telecommunications Europe Report "Strong recruitment and motivation results", April 2004)*

1.3 Emerging issues in leadership

Although the results of the MIS survey (Table 1.3) indicate that project management was not a top priority for IT directors, many companies in the UK and Europe are creating new permanent positions, such as "Director of Projects" or "Director–Project Delivery". These new posts indicate recognition of the fact that ongoing competitiveness is linked to project success and as such remains a significant management responsibility.

A research undertaken by McManus and Wood-Harper (2003) highlights that companies look for a number of potential skill sets in their project managers, the most important being a solid understanding of the business objectives. Also important was a level of respect within the organization and commitment to setting the "tone with senior management". These attributes should be taken into consideration when selecting project leaders. The role of project manager as a leader continues to evolve and vary across companies. For example, some project managers provide business and technical assurance to senior management, while others provide resources and domain knowledge to assist management in meeting their objectives. In essence project management can encompass many roles, acting in different capacities within different geographies and organizational units. This poses some significant questions and challenges for leadership. For example:

- What specific skill sets are necessary for leaders in project management?
- Does the organization have a compelling training and development programme for leaders in project management?
- Do leaders in project management have the capability to apply the latest thinking and techniques?

Emerging trends in project management and leadership point to a future where technical skills will have less currency than those associated with what is termed *human factor management*. A number of issues fitting this term are driving the way "best-of-breed organizations" train their project managers to carry out directives in their jurisdiction. This is not to negate the importance of technical skills and knowledge, but there is recognition that there is a greater need for skills in dealing with intrapersonal and interpersonal issues, particularly with stakeholders and senior levels of management.

In both the UK and USA, there is a large amount of research being done in various aspects of project leadership, for example, some of the aspects of research undertaken relate to:

- Team interaction (refer to Chapter 2)
- Decision making (refer to Chapter 3)
- Managing conflict in complex environments (refer to Chapter 4)
- Communication in complex environments (refer to Chapter 5)
- Leadership and governance (refer to Chapter 6).

In the USA significant research has been undertaken on issues associated with self-directed work teams. A report commissioned by the Project Management Institute has been used to identify key issues in decision making within this area. Research continues to indicate that many managers continue to perform at a fraction of their potential and creative best. The reasons most often cited include poor leadership, low emotional intelligence (EI) quotient competencies resulting in ineffective communications and poor relationships, and unresolved conflicts that are not addressed.

A key attribute of human factor management is EI. Leadership and management literature (see for instance Goleman, 1998) suggest that the most important factor distinguishing effective from ineffective leaders is their understanding and use of EI. A leader's EI includes the degree of self-awareness, and ability to manage emotions and engender self-motivation. EI also focuses on an individual's ability to relate well to others, be a mentor for others' emotional development, foster a motivating environment, and manage conflict effectively (a subject we will explore further in Chapter 4). One of the foundation skills for EI is the skill of empathy. It starts with self-awareness, in that understanding your own emotions is essential to understanding the feelings of others. It is crucial for effective communication and for leading others. Lack of empathy is a primary cause of interpersonal difficulties, leading to poor performance, project derailment, and problems with client and stakeholder relatio ships. In essence project leaders must be in tune with their EI, they must also to some degree act and be social architects, who understand the interaction of organizational and behavioural variables, who can foster a climate of active participation and can minimize dysfunctional conflict inside or outside the project.

1.4 Separating leadership from management

There is no universally agreed definition of management, so one definition is perhaps as good as another. My own view is that management is *"the process of achieving organizational goals by planning, organizing, and controlling organizational resources such as people and cash."*

Alternatively in project management, management may be described as "the activity consisting of those tasks that are performed to ensure that the mission of a project is fulfilled by planning and controlling its scope, schedule, costs, resources, and communication".

What each of these definitions has in common is that "management" is by and large concerned with the control of resources and reporting back on how such resources have been used. The work undertaken by Henri Fayol in the early part of the 20th century is largely the foundation upon which the general principles of project management were built and in essence defines the structure by which many projects are still managed today.

Fayol's general principles of management are:

1. *Division of work:* tasks should be subdivided and employees should specialize in a limited set of tasks so that expertise is developed and productivity increased.
2. *Authority and responsibility:* authority is the right to give orders and entails the responsibility for enforcing them with rewards and penalties; authority should be matched with corresponding responsibility.

3. *Discipline:* is essential for the smooth running of business and is dependent on good leadership, clear and fair agreements, and judicious application of penalties.
4. *Unity of command:* for any action whatsoever, an employee should receive orders from one superior only; otherwise authority, discipline, order, and stability are threatened.
5. *Unity of direction:* a group of activities concerned with a single objective should be co-ordinated by a single plan under one head.
6. *Subordination of individual interest to general interest:* individual or group goals must not be allowed to over-ride those of the business.
7. *Remuneration of personnel:* may be achieved by various methods and the choice is important; it should be fair, encourage effort, and not lead to overpayment.
8. *Centralization:* the extent to which orders should be issued only from the top of the organization is a problem, which should take into account its characteristics such as size and capabilities of the personnel.
9. *Scalar chain:* communications should normally flow up and down the line of authority running from the top to the bottom of the organization, but sideways communication between those of equivalent rank in different departments can be desirable so long as superiors are kept informed.
10. *Order:* both materials and personnel must always be in their proper place; people must be suited to their posts, so there must be careful organization of work and selection of personnel.
11. *Equity:* personnel must be treated with kindness and justice.
12. *Stability of tenure of personnel:* rapid turnover of personnel should be avoided because of the time required for the development of expertise.
13. *Initiative:* all employees should be encouraged to exercise initiative within the limits imposed by the requirements of authority and discipline.
14. *Esprit de corps:* efforts must be made to promote harmony within the organization and prevent dissension and divisiveness.

Although some of Fayol's principles (especially 1, 2, 4, 5, 9, and 10) continue to find favour amongst project managers, some of them are counter-productive to leadership. For example, Fayol advocates subordination of the individual to general interest, involving constant supervision. The total absence of team building, training, delegation, empowerment, and socialization from Fayol's model is a key attribute in the delivery of successful projects. In Fayol's model management, focus is directed at the time, cost, and quality paradigm. In support of this paradigm many organizations implement management processes to expose, integrate, transform, and connect disjointed information feedback systems and processes. Such intentions are good, but only rarely do organizations achieve long-term, meaningful, and sustainable results – ask any veteran project manager who has been involved in a "failed" project. Projects have a life of their own: they grow, join, change, shrink, and split, representing the ever-changing face of customer expectations. Projects also have a life cycle of change, not only in state (data), but also in structure (capability) and design (intention). For these reasons, companies need adaptable project managers who can think outside this time, cost, and quality paradigm. In today's arena for economic growth, organizational sustainability, and process innovation, companies need leaders, not just managers.

(See Henri Fayol, General and Industrial Management: translated by Constance Storrs (New York: Pitman, 1949) 5–6, 43–110).

Douglas McGregor wrote in *The Human Side of Enterprise*, "it was widely believed that leadership was a property of the individual that a limited number of people were uniquely endowed with abilities and traits which made it possible for them to become leaders. Moreover, these abilities and traits were believed to be inherited rather than acquired." Research undertaken by Bennis, McLean, and Covey argue that leaders possess different attributes and have a different focus. These authors see a distinction between the style of leaders and managers according to their primary focus. The respective positions of leaders and managers on a number of issues are listed in Table 1.4.

In practice, project managers need to adopt different styles to suit the environment and situation they find themselves in – the line between manager and leader is forever being redefined. One attribute a leader must possess is that of seeing the "bigger picture"; doing things right is not good enough, the project manager "must" do the right thing. Contemporary writers on the subject of leadership such as Bennis, Kouzes, Peters, and Posner, argue that leaders who do not possess this holistic ability are likely to have short-lived careers. According to Bennis, exemplary leaders in the 21st century will be distinguished by their mastery of skills in taste (the ability to cultivate talent), judgement, and character (1999).

Table 1.4 Management vs leadership styles

Management focus	Leadership focus
Goals and objectives	Vision
Telling how and when	Selling what and why
Shorter range	Longer range
Organization and structure	People
Autocracy	Democracy
Restraining	Enabling
Maintaining	Developing
Conforming	Challenging
Imitating	Originating
Administrating	Innovating
Directing and controlling	Inspiring trust
Procedures	Policy
Consistency	Flexibility
Risk avoidance	Risk opportunity
Bottomline	Topline

To some degree, leadership is an improvisional art in that many project managers operate in dynamic environments, where the rules can change in days, not weeks. In my experience, successful project managers engender trust, are adaptable, and are able to forge new collaborative relationships for themselves, their teams, and their ever-shifting portfolio of stakeholders.

1.4.1 Action centred leadership

In the 1980s, John Adair created a model of leadership based on his experiences of working with army personnel at the Sandhurst Military College. Professor Adair maintains that leadership is about teamwork, creating teams, and empowering people to results. Adair's Action Centred Leadership (ACL) model is based on three overlapping circles – task, team, and individual. Each interacts with the other two, so that failure, for example, to complete a task, or the lack of one, affects both the sense of team achievement and that of the individual.

Professor Adair's ACL model finds favour with project managers and their employing organizations because it embraces the meta skills of technical creativity and problem solving that project managers and their peers tend to value. Adair's ACL model demonstrates the three main areas a leader must attend to if a task is to be achieved with maximum satisfaction (see Figure 1.1). Adair has refined the ACL model to identify a number of attributes associated with leadership that are arguably fundamental to the management of projects. They are:

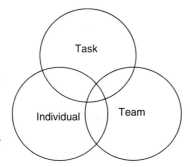

Figure 1.1
Adair's action centred leadership model (after Adair, 1983).

- *Planning:* seeking available information, defining group tasks or goals, making a workable plan.
- *Initiating:* briefing the group, allocating tasks, setting group standards.
- *Controlling:* maintaining group standards, ensuring progress towards objects, prodding actions and decisions.
- *Supporting:* expressing acceptance of individual contributions, encouraging and disciplining, creating team spirit, relieving tension with humour, reconciling disagreements.
- *Informing:* clarifying task and plan, keeping the group informed, receiving information from the group, summarizing ideas and suggestions.
- *Evaluating:* checking feasibility of ideas, testing consequence, evaluating group performance, helping the group to evaluate itself.

This model leadership approach, developed by Adair, has been successfully adopted by many project-based organizations, including GE, IBM, Microsoft, and Logica to name but a few. Adair's crucial contribution was not so much in identifying the three components of leadership (task, team, and the individual) as in insisting that they are interdependent. As suggested, it is impossible to satisfy objective (task) needs without adequate attention to team and individual needs. Similarly, team and individual needs are closely interlinked: the leader cannot adequately deal with one without also attending to the other.

1.5 Competencies and skills of leadership

Adair firmly believed that that leadership skills (and competencies) could be acquired through training and learning. Individual development is without doubt a differentiator when it comes to promotional choices amongst the junior and middle ranks of management, and many European organizations today see leadership training as an investment for the future. Creating the conditions under which potential leaders will flourish is paramount to the competitiveness of many organizations.

According to Peter Drucker, leadership requires aptitude, and people who are good program managers, technical architects, or database designers are rare enough in the software industry even without aptitude for leadership. Leadership also requires basic attitudes, and although many researchers have tried, nothing is as difficult to define and change as basic attitudes. With respect to aptitudes, a trend is emerging within project structured organizations that the required traits of project leaders appear to be coaching, insight, and multicultural management qualities such as establishing bridges, fruitful stakeholder relationships (cultural bridging skills), and remotely managing teams working in several different countries on one or more projects (Botten and McManus, 1999). This said, successful leadership is not solely dependent on the possession of a single trait or skill. Research findings to date suggest leadership is not a universal model of features possessed by some individuals but should be viewed more as a relationship between leader and events, which may have a political, economical, technical, or sociological dimension. In addition, research studies emphasize the importance of leadership skills and attitudes that can be acquired and are, therefore, not inborn characteristics of the individual. If we accept this point of view that leadership consists of a relationship between the leader and the event dimension, and if we recognize that these situational events are subject to substantial changes with time, we must recognize that both project managers and leaders are in the business of managing risk (McManus, 2003).

Writing in *Managing the Non-Profit Organisation* (1990), Peter Drucker, argued that leaders who worked most effectively never used the word "I". Leaders, he suggested, do not think "I". They think "we", they think "team". They understand their job is to make the team function. They accept the responsibility and do not sidestep it, but "we" gets the credit. There is an identification (very often, unconscious) with the task and with the group. This is what creates trust and what enables project managers to get the task done. Drucker identifies four key competencies associated with leadership. They are:

A willingness to listen
A willingness to communicate
A willingness not to alibi yourself
A willingness to realize how unimportant you are compared
to the task.

Having spent half of my working life in project management, I strongly identify with the last of these competencies. Project managers need to have objectivity, a certain detachment. According to Drucker, they subordinate themselves to the project (task), but do not identify themselves with the project. The project remains both bigger than they are and different. The worst thing you can say about a project manager (leader) is that on the day he or she left, the project collapsed. When that happens, it means the so-called project manager has sucked the place dry. They have not built. They may have been effective operators, but they have not created.

1.5.1 Leadership skills

Within the global software industry and in most of the software-related organizations, project managers tend to hold positions of influence and be opinion leaders. Successful (or otherwise) project managers are likely to be self-starters and depict many of the action-oriented roles (shaper, implementer, and completer finisher) described by Meredith Belbin (2003). Characteristics associated with these role types include descriptions such as dynamic, challenging, courageous, decisive, integrity, disciplined, reliable, efficient, practical, someone who has high energy and overcomes obstacles. In many respects these are qualities found and associated with entrepreneurs. According to John Kotter, people who provide effective leadership always seem to have above-average energy levels, often much above average. They appear to thrive on achieving something important and being in a position of influencing others to achieve. This inner drive is often associated with high personal standards, certain dissatisfaction with the status quo, and a tendency to push for continuing improvements (Kotter, 1990).

For those engaged in software projects, intellectual skills and social abilities are particularly important to direction setting. Projects over their life cycle generate a lot of paperwork and information. Project managers need the ability to understand diverse business and technical information – sensing relevant patterns in information requires a set of skills of significant cognitive ability. Projects also have stakeholders, so skills such as communication, advocacy, negotiation, public relations, diplomacy, and the ability to motivate are also crucial. In my experience, few project managers have proven themselves as leaders or go the distance without demonstrating most of these skills (see Table 1.5).

Table 1.5 Summaries: competencies and leadership skills for project managers

Leading change (must have/be)	Leading people (must have/be)	Performance driven (must have/be)	Domain expertise (must have/be)	Building alliances (must have/be)
Vision	Integrity and honesty	Accountable	Financial and technical acumen	Political acumen
Open to continued learning	Team builder	Customer focused		Influencer
Flexibility	Conflict manager	Decisive		Negotiator
Resilience	Leverage diversity	Problem solver		Communicator
External awareness		Entrepreneur		
Motivation				
Strategic thinker				

1.6 Followership and leadership

Project managers cannot lead effectively if they have not first learned how to follow. Ineffective followers have trouble distinguishing when it is time to follow and when to lead. For the majority of project managers acquiring "competencies and skills" is an incremental process and without exception those project managers who acquire star and leadership status would have been followers at some point in their careers. Leadership begins with great followership. Exemplary leaders walk in the footsteps of previous leaders. They can look back on their lives and quickly recount those who mentored them, and who acted and modelled great leadership for them.

Many academics argue that the principal breakthrough in leadership theory came when James McGregor Burns introduced the concept of "transformational leadership" in his classic, Pulitzer Prize-winning book titled, simply, *Leadership*. Burns explained that most leaders are "transactional" with their followers, that is, they offer something in exchange for allegiance, for example, promotion. Transformational leadership on the other hand is different. It is considered more complex. According to Burns, the transforming leader recognizes an existing need or demand of a potential follower. But, beyond that, the transforming leader looks for potential motives in followers, seeks to satisfy higher needs, and engages the full person of the follower. Table 1.6 identifies the leadership traits of transactional and transformational leaders.

Table 1.6 Leadership traits

Transactional leadership	Transformational leadership
• Contingent reward	• Idealized influence
• Constructive	• Charisma
• Transactions	• Inspirational
• Management by exception	• Motivational
• Active and passive	• Intellectual stimulation
• Corrective transactions	• Individualized consideration

Transformational leadership behaviour traits

• Sets strong role model
• Demonstrates emotional intelligence
• Demonstrates competence
• Articulates goals
• Communicates high expectations
• Expresses confidence
• Arouses motives

Transformational leadership effects on followers

• Trust leader's ideology
• Belief in similarity between leader and follower
• Unquestioning acceptance
• Obedience
• Identification with leader
• Emotional involvement
• Heightened goals
• Increased confidence

As is obvious, followers are the ones who experience the actuality of a project manager's approach to leadership and are uniquely able to evaluate it and its effects. According to Hollander, whether called *transactional* or *transformational leaders,* the common elements shown in good leadership, and not in bad, are such significant relational factors as intangible rewards. The view held by Hollander is that transformational leadership can be seen as an extension of transactional leadership, in which there is greater leader intensity and follower arousal. This amounts to having a large fund of credits accorded to the leader by followers, thereby granting esteem and more sway in being influential. Finally, to achieve a response following it is essential at the outset to establish and build upon transactional leadership before expecting an adequate response to transformational leadership.

Project managers who have built teams and led teams know from experience that you cannot always take the lead. Some times it is prudent (and common sense) to let followers take the lead in initiatives; not only does this help in their personal development, but it also helps build trust and confidence between the project manager and those who follow. Followers want leaders who are knowledgeable, can maintain momentum, bring and create energy, and pay attention to the needs of all. Project managers with high EI understand the people who follow them, why they are there, and what is in it for them. Tom Peters in *Thriving on Chaos* put it concisely: "The most effective leaders empower others to act and grow in support of a course of action that both leaders and followers find value in – to this end communication is a powerful tool." Alternatively, Larry Cowen puts it like this:

> *I have found that a formal leadership role can often block effective, honest communication. Too often, people are unwilling to take the risk and educate the leader about what is 'really' going on. The only effective way to break this down is for leaders to place themselves in the follower role as you have described it, thus placing others in the leader role so that the knowledge inside them can be surfaced and acted upon.*

> *I also believe that follower skills are needed to recognize the potential in others. As a leader, a significant part of the job is enabling others to lead, and lead well. The secret is to pick the right people for the right job. This is not an easy task if done well. A new leader must be placed in an environment that provides them a good opportunity for success; something to build upon. Follower skills help a leader recognize the leadership qualities in others. Follower skills also help a leader identify opportunities that are best matched with the individual.*

> *(Source: Larry Cowen, Vice President, Corporate and Technology Planning, Preserver Group, Inc., USA)*

1.7 Building teams

Projects are not delivered solely by project managers – they are based on the accumulated efforts of individual followers. As previously suggested, an effective project manager needs to be a competent "social architect". Going back to the Adair ACL model, to be effective, the project manager must identify major issues associated with task, team, and individual. In the main, these will be team related with emphasis on behavioural aspects such as team structure, trust and respect, or barriers to team development and so on; project task and resource related such as goals and objectives, planning and scope management, and organizational. The latter will include organizational development and involve stakeholders to ensure visibility, resource availability, and overall support for the project throughout its life cycle.

According to Batten, there are five things that members of a successful team need from their leader: expectation, opportunity, feedback, guidance and reward. Given these prerequisites, both the followers and their leader can be expected to progress and develop interactively. The leader focuses successively on telling, selling, gelling, and producing project activities, in which the ideal is for the team to become a self-directed work team (a subject we will discuss in Chapter 2). This will only occur as a result of careful team development and typically advances interactively through three distinct stages of team building and evolution. According to George Graen, these three stages of team development are characterized as:

1. Initial
2. Mentoring
3. Normalization.

Before going on to discuss each of these stages, I would like briefly to say something about the leader's role and tasks within this three-stage process. When the team forms, the leader's main concern is to familiarize the team with the skills needed to undertake the task. In this situation the leader must focus on the wider issues and adopt a telling leadership style. During the three-stage process the leader should maintain a high profile and involve team members in the decision process. To some extent this engagement process will involve the leader adopting different styles during each of the three stages. In the latter stage the leader's focus will drop from task mentoring to concentrate on relationships (Table 1.7).

1.7.1 The initial managing stage

During this time, the project manager instructs and assesses team members in the usual way: tasks are assigned and outcomes observed. Over time, the project manager notes that some staff perform well, while others are undependable. Among those who perform well, some seem to adopt the project manager's own approach naturally, that is, they make the same decisions, take the same actions, and value the same outcomes. In general, they come to think and act like the project manager. Consequently, the project manager becomes steadily more comfortable in delegating

Table 1.7 Stages of project leadership and followership team development

	Initial	Mentoring	Normalization
Leader	• Advises team members • Delegates responsibility • Initiates most of the interactions	• Acts as pastor • Shares information • Builds confidence • Builds awareness	• Formalized relationship • Respect • Friendship • Trust established
Follower	• Takes advice • Follows instructions • Builds trust • Demonstrates talent	• Takes initiative • Suggests solutions • Takes on responsibility • Builds on relationships	• Formalized relationship • Respect • Friendship • Trust established

responsibility to these people. This means that they move into the core group, especially if they are psychologically compatible with the project manager, that is, if friendship comes easily. In this stage, the project manager usually initiates most of the interactions that take place. For most team members, a relationship with the project manager never advances beyond this stage since the interactions tend to be businesslike, dictated by the formal role each person is assigned. However, for those individuals with whom the project manager feels comfortable, who share "similar motivations", and especially those who have some particular talent or characteristic needed by the project manager, the relationship ripens into the second stage.

1.7.2 The mentoring stage

One easily recognizable feature of this stage is a tendency for team members to take more initiative by acting as a project manager in terms of initiating projects, suggesting solutions, and taking on responsibility. The follower begins to share in some of the action and excitement of the project managerial role, being privy to inside information, exercising more flexibility in work assignments, and feeling the frustrations involved in allocating power and resources. The relationship between the project manager and the team member can now be better understood by considering the project manager as a mentor and the follower as a pupil project manager. If the relationship continues to grow and expand, if the apprentice project manager continues to help the mentor solve larger and larger problems, if the organizational resources allow it, and if the two people see it as in their best interests, a third stage appears, the normalization stage.

1.7.3 The normalization stage

Here the special relationship becomes normal, and perhaps even formalized in the organizations structure and in its policy manual. Junior project managers tend to become special assistants, or receive some other formal title, being recognized as individuals with power in their own right, even as their special relationship with the project manager continues. In this way, the programmer becomes an analyst and the bright young analyst becomes a project leader. Their special relationships with the project manager become engraved on the organizational scroll. Hopefully, of course, the personal friendships continue to grow and flourish also.

1.8 Chapter summary – 10 key points

The most important points to take away from this chapter are:

1. Leadership will become the central driver of the 21st century, and the future state of project management is now tied to the leadership, stakeholder, and risk management paradigm.
2. Leadership is about the mix of "vision and the ability" to guide people to ensure that they all try and meet the objective as a team.
3. Motivation is important to the success of any project undertaking because it is essentially about winning the hearts and minds of people. It is also clear that what may be characterized as project "management" is equally important because this is about getting things done.
4. One of the prime challenges faced by project managers is that of getting people to accept responsibility for their own actions and take ownership of risk. Often project managers have to use a plethora of emotional, motivational, and reward strategies for different people – taken at face value this may be considered a useful approach to achieving objectives, however, it is time consuming and in many instances counter-productive to team building.
5. Emerging trends in project management and leadership point to a future where technical skills will have less currency than those associated with "human factor management". This is not to negate the importance of technical skills and knowledge, but there is recognition that there is a greater need for skills in dealing with intrapersonal and interpersonal issues, particularly with stakeholders and senior levels of management.
6. Projects have a life of their own: they grow, join, change, shrink, and split, representing the ever-changing face of

customer expectations. Projects also have a life cycle of change, not only in state (data), but also in structure (capability) and design (intention). For these reasons, companies need adaptable project managers who can think outside this time, cost, and quality paradigm.

7. Project managers need to adopt different styles to suit the environment and situation they find themselves in – the line between manager and leader is forever being redefined.

8. Project managers need the ability to understand diverse business and technical information – sensing relevant patterns in information requires a set of skills of significant cognitive ability. Projects also have stakeholders, so skills such as communication, advocacy, negotiation, public relations, diplomacy, and the ability to motivate are also crucial.

9. Project managers cannot lead effectively if they have not first learned how to follow. Those who have built and led teams know from experience that you cannot always take the lead. Sometimes it is prudent (and common sense) to let followers take the lead in initiatives – not only does this help in their personal development but it helps build trust and confidence between the project manager and those who follow.

10. Projects are not delivered solely by project managers; they are based on the accumulated efforts of individual followers. As previously suggested, an effective project manager needs to be a competent social architect.

1.9 Next chapter

In the next chapter we will explore some of the concepts and ideas outlined in this chapter – specifically we will examine "leadership and team development" and debate the issues related to creating high-performance teams, empowering, objective setting, coaching and mentoring, and measuring and rewarding project teams. We will also debate the relatively new and emerging concept of self-directed work teams.

Chapter references

Belbin, R.M. (2003) Management Teams: Why They Succeed or Fail (second edition). Oxford, Butterworth-Heinemann.

Botten, N. and J. McManus (1999) Competitive Strategies for Service Organizations. Hampshire, Macmillan Press.

Goleman, D. (1998) Working with Emotional Intelligence: Why It Can Matter More Than IQ. Bantam Books.

Kotter, J. (1990) A Force for Change. New York, Free Press.

Kouzes, J.M. and B.Z. Posner (1987) The Leadership Challenge: How to Get Extraordinary Things Done in Organizations. San Francisco, Ca, Jossey-Bass Publishing.

McManus, J. (2001) Risk in software projects, management services. 45, 6–10.

McManus, J. (2003) Risk Management in Software Development Projects, Oxford, Elsevier, Butterworth-Heinemann.

McManus, J. and T. Wood-Harper (2003) Information Systems Project Management: Methods, Tools and Techniques, Upper Saddle River, NJ, Pearson Education (Prentice Hall).

Further reading

Adair, J. (1983) Effective Leadership: A Self-development Manual. Hampshire, Gower Press.

Adair, J. (1988) Understanding Motivation. London, Talbart and Adair Press.

Adair, J. (1990) Developing Leaders. London, Talbart and Adair Press.

Aryanpur, S. (2004) Reading between the lines. Managing Information Strategies, April, 42–43.

Batten, J.D. (1989) Tough-Minded Leadership AMACOM 1989.

Bennis, W. (1989) On Becoming a Leader. Boston, MA, Addison Wesley.

Bennis, W. (1999) The Leadership Advantage. Leader-to-Leader No. 12, spring.

Covey, S.R. (1991) Principle-Centred Leadership. Quezon City, Philippines, Summit Books.

Drucker, P.F. (1990) Managing the Non-Profit Organisation. Oxford, Butterworth-Heinemann.

Graen, G.B. and M. Uhl-Bien (1994) Team leadership-making theory: from mature dyads grow high performance teams. In Handbook of Leadership, Kieser, A., Reber, G. and R. Wunderer (Eds) Vol. II, Kenstrasse, FRG, C.E. Paeschel Verlag.

Hollander, E.P. (1997) How and Why Active Followers Matter in Leadership, Working Papers. College Park, MD, Academy of Leadership Press.

Kouzes, J.M. and B.Z. Posner (2002) The Leadership Practices Inventory: Theory and Evidence Behind the Five Practices of Exemplary Leaders.

McGregor, D. (1960) The Human Side of Enterprise. New York, McGraw-Hill.

McGregor, J.B. (1978) Leadership. New York, Harper and Row.

McLean, J.W. and W. Weitzel (1991) Leadership: Magic, Myth or Method? AMACOM.

Leadership and Team Development

2.1 Building high-performance teams

It was stated in Chapter 1 (Section 1.7) that: *"projects are not delivered solely by project managers; they are based on the accumulated efforts of individual followers."* Individual followers make up teams and good teamwork is an unbeatable advantage when it comes to delivering software projects. Research undertaken by Warren Bennis shows that many teams are only half or less than half, as effective as they ought to be – in contrast, high-performance teams (HPT) produce performances that just get better and better.

Project managers have an obligation to sow the seeds of success – their aim is to create teams that achieve extraordinary performance. In his book *Organizing Genius*, Bennis examined groups of people who have achieved extraordinary and revolutionary results working together. What Bennis learned from observing these HPT was that:

- The right person has the right job.
- Its members are likely to help each other succeed.
- They have an effective leader or manager.
- They are filled with people who get along.
- They know that they belong to something special.
- Individuals get recognition as part of team accomplishment.
- They are tight-knit groups with healthy links to the rest of the world.
- They always have an enemy external to themselves (an enemy can be something tangible as a competitor or as intangible as crime).
- They deliver; they are accountable for deliverables. They run things, recommend things, or make or do things together.
- They believe that ?excellence is its own reward.

People who work in HPT also demonstrate above-average energy levels; members appear to succeed on achieving high levels of performance in difficult situations. This inner drive is often associated with high personal standards and dissatisfaction with the status quo. HPT often look to their project managers for evidence of values-driven leadership usually because they have seen too many examples of people in positions of authority who are self-serving, focussed only on financial results, or simply indifferent to others and quick to apportion blame.

Given the rate of worldwide project failures, many project managers operate in environments where "blame culture" is high and moral is low. One of the characteristics of HPT is that whilst striving for excellence, they induce zero tolerance to blame cultures – as Ronald Klein observes:

> Great Groups, while striving for excellence, create an atmosphere where "mistakes" are not only tolerated but encouraged since they are markers on the path to greatness. This gives the group members the freedom to move beyond safe traditional boundaries and suggest "unorthodox" creative, perhaps playful alternatives for problem solving. It also leads to personal growth for group members.
>
> (Source: Dr Ronald M. Klein, in conversation with Warren Bennis, Thursday, April 3, 1997)

As discussed in the previous chapter, a powerful way to foster team building is to be a positive communicator. One way to exemplify teamwork in HPT is to reveal important information about intent relative to the teams work. As a result of this action, team members usually follow suit. A project manager's self-disclosure fosters trust as it leads to shared perceptions and concerns. The important thing to note here is that whilst interacting with team members, the project manager can emphasize that they are also part of the team.

Individuals who work within HPT often see themselves as catalysts. As stated, they expect to achieve a great deal, but are aware that they can do little without the efforts of other project stakeholders. HPT engage their stakeholder communities and encourage active participation in the decision-making process (a point we will return to in Chapter 3); they also inspire and empower stakeholders to take responsibility for their own actions and behaviour.

2.1.1 High-performance teams and motivation

Project managers are responsible for the well-being of their team. In software engineering projects, team members are drawn from various disciplines, for example, they could be system designers, programmers, quality engineers, support engineers, and so on. Bringing together a group of professionals and forging them into an HPT not only takes leadership but requires continuous motivation on the project manager's part. The motivational aspects of management are often stressed by academics of business in many postgraduate business classes. It can be argued that all problems in management are people problems. From designing software to poor client relations, people are the only one who can fix problems. When we emphasize what a project manager needs to do to motivate professional employees, we sometimes miss the problem. Although crucial, project managers do not always deal well with the self-esteem and self-actualization needs of their team. Many project managers are by nature systematic and goal-oriented. This can be considered a good thing when the goals of others are recognized and encouraged. Too often, however, the need for others to achieve goals is overlooked.

It is acknowledged that there have been questions and refinements to the works of Maslow and Herzberg; they are, however, still the most widely recognized and cited authors of motivation. Herzberg and Maslow state that motivation begins with needs. If needs are unsatisfied, we establish a goal, either consciously or unconsciously, and take action to achieve that goal. There are, of course, exceptions to this view – some people simply do not take any action towards goals at all. Often, in fact, bad work experiences tend to diminish the ability even to perceive a goal, let alone formulate plans to reach it, however, simplistic they may be. Some individuals (or team members) of this kind pay a high price for their inability to participate in goal objectives, even suffering complete alienation within the team. This in itself shows the profoundly deep-rooted relevance of goals: those who do not share the team consensus of their importance can risk isolation from the organization itself.

There is substantial consistency in human performance. Like others, project managers want to succeed in whatever they attempt. For project managers, success tends to become habitual, just as winning races becomes habitual for athletes. According to Dawson, one of the most important and well-established organizational findings related to performance is that people tend to perform at roughly the same level as those people who are close to them. Groups of people working together (whether analysts, programmers, testers, etc.) set up informal norms of performance. These norms tend to be reinforced, usually in subtle ways, by the members of the group. Software developers, for example, usually reach an unstated understanding of how much work they consider to be fair. The group subtly disciplines any developer who becomes overeager and attempts to exceed this norm. Such individuals are brought into line so as not to embarrass the rest of the group by showing them up. Good leaders should possess situational awareness that helps them tune into delicate and emerging situations. A good leader should establish standards that the team, as a whole, has empathy with.

Returning to the topic of motivation, Maslow argued that people have "basic needs" that must be met in order for them to feel fulfiled. Maslow arranged these needs into a series of levels according to their importance. The first level, for example, was termed "biological needs" and referred to requirements such as food, water, and shelter. Higher level needs included transcendence (helping others to find fulfilment) and self-actualization (achieving a person's full potential). Traditionally, project managers have sought to meet only the lower level needs of their staff. Often, project managers have concentrated on issues such as performance at the expense of other needs, such as helping people to develop their capabilities. The importance of esteem and self-fulfilment should not be underestimated. Most Human Resource Departments can recount cases where highly talented members of staff have moved elsewhere to find more challenging and rewarding work or because they felt undervalued.

In creating high-performance project teams, it is not enough for the project manager to act as the person who sets goals and enforces certain standards of behaviour. Herzberg referred to the factors causing dissatisfaction as "hygiene factors", using the analogy that hygiene does not improve health, but does prevent sickness. Herzberg was able to identify a set of factors, which act as true motivators, making lasting fulfilment and commitment possible. These are:

- A sense of achievement from completing work
- Recognition from others within the organization
- Responsibility assumed
- Varied work, interesting tasks, and
- Promotion prospects.

(Source: Frederick Herzberg, Work and the Nature of Man, Staples Press, USA, 1968)

What implications do the theories of Maslow and Herzberg have for project managers? Implicit in Maslow and Herzberg higher order needs is the desire for achievement or accomplishment.

For example, in his theory, Maslow highlighted the importance of intrinsic motivation: this is the motivation stemming from the individual, which raises questions (for the project manager) on how work might be structured to facilitate individual satisfaction of higher order needs. Conversely extrinsic motivation results from factors external to the individual, for example, pay, which Herzberg classifies as a lower order need or hygiene factor.

Whilst the absence of these motivators will not necessarily cause team members to resign, an increase in their strength will lead directly to increased individual fulfilment. In turn, this will lead to sustained or higher levels of performance. It is important to remember that team members are unique individuals and what is acceptable to one person may not be to another. This simple truth is what makes motivation an interesting academic problem. Although many would argue the contrary, we cannot evolve a panacea to motivational problems for each problem would need an ongoing analysis of the individual team member. As a former senior manager with General Electric, my experience leads me to conclude that the different motivational needs of people are often difficult to predict – one thing I have learned in my management career is that to motivate teams to high performance, you have to set "high standards" for yourself and lead by example and deeds.

2.2 Empowering teams

For many academics and practitioners alike the literature has lacked consensus on a definition of empowerment. In essence, notions of empowerment are derived from theories of participative management and employee involvement. Theories of participative management advocate that managers share decision-making power with employees to enhance performance and work satisfaction. Theories of employee involvement emphasize cascading power, information, rewards, and training to the lowest level possible in the organizational hierarchy to increase worker discretion.

In the classic theoretical work on empowerment, Thomas and Velthouse (1990) conceptualized empowerment as the gestalt[i] of four cognitions: a sense of meaning, competence, self-determination, and impact. These dimensions are not predictors or outcomes of

---

[i] A set of elements such as a person's thoughts and experiences considered as a whole and regarded as amounting to more than the sum of its parts.

empowerment, but rather comprise its very essence. Meaning or purpose involves a fit between the needs of one's work role and one's values, beliefs, and behaviours. Competence or self-efficacy is a belief that one possesses the skills and abilities necessary to perform a job or task well and is analogous to agency beliefs, personal mastery, or effort–performance expectancy. Self-determination is the belief that one has autonomy or control over how one does his or her own work.

Writing in the *Journal of Extension*, Page and Czuba (1999) maintain that empowerment is a process that challenges "our" assumptions about the way things are and can be. It challenges our basic assumptions about power, helping, achieving, and succeeding. To begin to demystify the concept of empowerment, we need to understand the concept broadly in order to be clear about how and why we narrow our focus of empowerment for specific programmes and projects (specific dimension or level, etc.) and to allow discussion of empowerment across disciplinary and practice lines. Understanding empowerment becomes a critical issue for all project managers.

The rationale for empowerment approaches in project management is very compelling and arises from an increasing recognition that project managers do not hold a monopoly on technical knowledge or wisdom, and to sustain satisfaction and motivation there needs to be a greater role for the team followers in the social, economic, and political spheres that shape the project and their careers. The practice, however, indicates that little has changed in involving the stakeholder communities in any meaningful way, in project planning, design, or implementation. For example, the survey undertaken in 2004 by *MIS* (Table 1.3) makes little mention of participation. Likewise the Templeton College, Oxford Survey notes that its evaluations have found that participation had not gone much beyond relatively superficial information and consultation processes in the majority of projects (Table 1.1).

If we accept that empowerment encompasses far more than meeting the time, cost, and quality paradigm objectives, this has implications for how an empowerment programme might be carried out. Empowerment in this context lies in the relationship with the team, stakeholders, and institutions with which the project interact, and how these entities influence this relationship. Although not 100% guaranteed, the outcomes of these interactions are a raised level of personal empowerment for economic action and a redistribution of resources and decision making. For example, within the National Health Service (NHS) project interventions for empowerment often target nonclinicians who are often the most disempowered in the project stakeholder community setting due to factors related to clinical dominance. These interventions are generally based on the time, cost, and quality paradigm that assumes the most appropriate path to empowerment lies in overcoming time or resource constraints and that there is an immediate economic priority in people's lives, which is generally not the case.

2.3 A model for empowerment

A major attribute of empowerment is to promote the attitude among group members that working together and encouraging each other is an expected standard of team work. Developing a norm for empowering individuals can be difficult especially where a culture of centralization exists within an organization. Some project managers encourage team members to follow a model of empowerment that involves Encouragement, Engagement, and Enablement (or the 3Es, see Figure 2.1).

The triad model outlined in Figure 2.1 is a powerful but simplistic mechanism for a leader to promote empowerment and to exemplify team work. Encouraging people within the team to play a more active role in their work usually requires the project manager to tread a fine line between challenging the team members and creating competition. For example, when encouraging competition with other project groups the project manager should encourage rivalry, not intense competition that might lead to unethical business practices and a total loss of cooperation.

There are two potential pitfalls to take into consideration when implementing participatory and empowerment approaches to

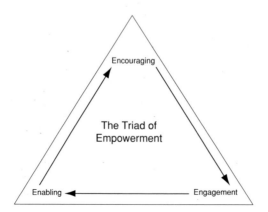

Figure 2.1
Triad model of
empowerment.

managing projects. The first of these is that engaging the disaffected is often a far more difficult task than engaging the more powerful stakeholder groups. It is fairly easy to demonstrate to project sponsors for instance why their participation in a particular initiative would be valuable. It is not the same for the disaffected and therefore different strategies are required to achieve one's aim. For this reason, empowerment approaches usually involve the project manager working on the ground and not on paper. The second thing to consider is that for empowerment to work effectively, the project manager must be prepared to change and learn to accept change. The main changes are:

- *Loss of power:* the project manager should be prepared to accept a loss of power.
- *Learn to listen:* the project manager should be prepared to listen actively and not pay lip service.
- *Loss of control:* the project manager should be prepared to concede control to the project community so that they own the project or initiative. All these are crucial, if participation is to succeed.

2.4 Self-directed work teams

As previously stated, there is some evidence to suggest that project management standards and those organizations that employ project managers do not value the leadership characteristics needed for excellent projects and instead attract applicants to the discipline who have a strong motivation for quantitative analysis in lieu of interpersonal skills so badly needed for empowering and building HPT.

In the 1990s, I worked in software industry managing and delivering numerous software systems for "blue chip" clients. Part of my duties involved the training and coaching of project managers. During this period, I observed that few individuals were able or interested in the stakeholder and political side of project management. I also became aware of an increasing number of projects that were under threat because management had placed a square peg in a round hole (this is typically symptomatic in system integration practices – where resource managers [in the main nonvalue adding individuals] take the next available person without much or any thought to the skills fit).

In the software industry, separating the discipline of project management from project manager can be difficult. All too often the two are used interchangeably. This is partly due to the insistence of the industry following projects standards such as PRINCE2. It is also due to the persistence of the hierarchical, no-participatory project structures that have provided a single-point scapegoat in the person of a project manager at the cost of multipoint participant contributions. All too often the role of managing internal and external stakeholders is left out of the equation. There is an emerging school of thought, which suggests that stakeholder management and client relations are too important to lump with the already full list of project management duties and that the task of project management should be distributed – just as total quality management (TQM) is in many production organizations.

One of the fundamental building blocks of TQM is its reliance on the use of self-directed work teams (SDWT). One of the most respected organizations in the world the Juran Institute advocates that SDWT require commitments that will change an organization's structure, management practices, and compensation systems and personnel policies.

In a project context, SDWT are generally multiskilled personnel who share responsibilities for producing a particular product or service. The subtle difference between SDWT and HPT previously discussed is that SDWT possess full empowerment of responsibility and results (task, time, cost, and quality) – which is not always the case with HPT. In essence, SDWT are a logical step in the evolution of empowerment. As suggested, participative teams and shared leadership teams are usually empowered to do their work, to make the decisions needed to satisfy their customers' requirements, and to operate with little or no management intervention. Another characteristic of SDWT is that they are not in it for the short term. They generally stay together for a long period of time even when a project is concluded rather than disband the "team stays together" on an ongoing basis (again this can be an issue with resource and other line managers).

Although tied to strategic objectives of the organization, SDWT members typically create their own goals and schedules, play a larger role in ensuring product or service delivery and quality, participate in hiring and spending decisions, and deal with external suppliers. The adoption of SDWT generally leads to an increase in competitiveness. As many would attest, the software industry is a highly competitive business, so whatever gives you an edge in the business is worth protecting. One solid use of SDWT is in the software development cycle where continuity, experience, efficiency, and quality matters.

Although many large organizations have implemented SDWT (with varying degrees of success) like any management initiative using SDWT is no panacea, nor should it be. The decision to implement SDWT should not be taken lightly. The process typically takes 2–5 years to achieve and affects every aspect of organizational life. Project managers looking to influence their organizations to consider a conversion should have a clear purpose in mind. Namely, SDWT should enable a firm to meet its strategic business and project goals with minimum disruption and investment. One of the objectives of introducing SDWT should be to enhance behavioural change. For example, the social structure of SDWT should enhance behavioural change. Effective teams find ways for each individual to contribute and thereby gain distinction. The same team dynamics that promote improved performance also support learning more effectively than do larger organizational units or individuals working alone.

Mark Chatfield offers some good advice to those individuals or organizations thinking of implementing SDWT. His advice is as follows:

- To create SDWT, a demand for performance is more important than team-building exercises. You can get a group together and train them in teamwork for weeks but they will not be a team until they have a common understanding of the need to perform. First comes the strategic plan, then the tasks needed to carry out the plan, finally, teams are formed to do the tasks.
- SDWT basics are often overlooked. These basics are "size", purpose, goals, skills, approach, and accountability.
- SDWT at the top are the most difficult. Executives have complex, long-term challenges, heavy demands on their time, and they got where they are by being trouble shooters.
- There is no need to throw out the hierarchy altogether. SDWT are the best way to integrate across structural boundaries. They are the best way to design and energize core processes.
- SDWT permit performance and learning at the same time. There is no better way to become a learning organization than to have a team-based structure that thrives on people learning from peers.

(*Mark Chatfield is Vice President for Engineering Leadership, Interaction Research Institute, Inc., Fairfax, VA*)

To conclude this section, I would like to reinforce the point made by Mark Chatfield on team size. For the majority of projects, there is always an optimum team size and although team sizes

Table 2.1 Software development projects: example of team size model

Model 1	Model 2	Model 3
Small project	Medium project	Large project
Definition up to 500 function points	Definition up to 2500 function points	Definition above 2500 function points
Team size 5–8	Team size 15–20	Team size above 20
Little external involvement	Formal steering groups and multiple stakeholders	Formal steering groups, sublevel meetings, and multiple stake-holders, emphasis on risk
Quick, short-time scales, consensus among stakeholders	Key stakeholders on steering committee, deci-sions take longer, emphasis on when and how	As in model 2, but with steep learning curves, everyone wants to have a say.
Normally good chance of meeting original require-ments with little risk to provider	Normally delivered but over budget and under the original specification	Normally prone to failure

do vary, the vitality, creativity, and innovation needed should not. Although not absolute, Table 2.1 provides a view on team sizes for small-, large-, and medium-sized software development projects. The three models also provide some insight into these limitations.

2.5 Setting team objectives

Projects usually require direct or indirect input from a variety of internal and external people, including the customer, the providing team, managers, and a whole variety of stakeholders. Each will have a role to play (major or minor) in defining and determining the projects success. Each should have specific tasks and responsibilities that must be performed to achieve success. It has already been stated that project teams should be orientated towards objectives, which in many cases will only be a subset of the overall aims of the project. One duty of a project manager is to ensure that any subservient objectives do not threaten the achievement of the wider strategic aims from which the project is drawn. Projects are not instigated to motivate teams – projects should originate from a business need that exists for the customer. This business need must be the focus for all concerned and should form the nucleus upon which the project derives its objectives.

Since Peter Drucker wrote *The Practice of Management* in 1954, there have been more than 250 studies completed demonstrating repeated findings or "basic truths" about humans and objectives. Truths incorporated in repeated findings indicate that:

1. People accomplish beyond their historical norm when they use objectives.
2. People respond positively to stretch objectives that they judge to be reasonable or attainable.
3. People stay attached to objectives when leaders support a goal process by both modelling the goal-related behaviour and providing feedback relative to goal progress.

In project management, the single and most important constraint is "time" and time places demands on managers and team members alike and because time is at a premium, it is the measure by which many objectives are measured. In simplistic terms, objective setting is a six-stage process:

1. The business objectives must be stated clearly.
2. The project deliverables must be defined.
3. The tasks must be defined.
4. The performance measures must be defined.
5. The controls must be established.
6. The task objectives must be agreed and assigned to individual team members (some questions the project manager may ask here are: what skills or knowledge and behaviours are needed to ensure the individual meets the agreed objective?).

It is good practice when setting objectives to ensure clarity with respect to roles and responsibilities. It is also useful if they are SMART objectives (Table 2.2). One of the advantages of SMART objectives is that they are pointed; that is they have an edge, often a sense of energy created by the specificity, the time limits, and the management. *Non-SMART* objectives, for example, improve testing productivity but seem flat in comparison.

The main purpose of agreeing upon objectives is to ensure a gauge for accomplishment and contribution to the business objective. The secondary goal is to improve project performance and support the ongoing learning and development of the team members and to this end objectives should:

Table 2.2 SMART objectives

Specific	Objectives must express the action and results required so that both the staff member and supervisor can see clearly whether or not the objective has been achieved
Measurable	When setting objectives, there must be some way of measuring and verifying whether the objective has been achieved and to what level
Achievable	Although they should provide challenge and development to the individual, objectives also must be achievable
Realistic	The objectives must be relevant to the level at which the individual is at their career and to the priorities and workload of their particular area
Time bound	Objectives need to have clear time frames attached to them. Although the performance development and review process is annual, objectives can be set for longer time frames. This may be particularly appropriate for research-based objectives where objectives may be set for longer periods but reviewed at least on an annual basis

Promote an individual work planning environment linked to the goals of the work unit

Promote career planning and development

Provide at least an annual occasion to formally review goals, provide feedback on performance, and discuss broader issues that impact on the staff member's working life

Provide the basis for evaluative judgements to be made in relation to incremental advancement

Provide the framework for dealing with under-performance

Focus on coaching, mentoring, and support (see Section 2.7)

One of the key documents used in the process of software engineering is the customer requirement specification. In software engineering, requirements add to the objective definition while outlining definition and creating a set of boundaries for the development of an action plan. In addition, requirements ensure that when you deliver on the objective, the results will be satisfying to the customer.

2.6 Ownership of the objective

Research shows that teams perform better if they truly believe in and take ownership of the objectives. According to Sir John

Harvey-Jones (1998, *Making IT Happen*, p. 60), clarity of the objective and widespread knowledge of it only come from end-less repetition and endless iteration checking that the objective is still possible and relevant. Your people (*project team*) will be switched off the moment the objective that you have set appears to be unobtainable. They will strive and fight for an end, even if they think there is only small chance of success. But the stage at which they come to believe, there is no way in which they can achieve the aim is the stage at which you need to re-examine the objective that the business (*project*) has been set. You need, first of all, to have a sufficiently open system to know that this change has occurred, and second, to be willing to acknowledge the change, and go through the whole exercise again (*with your team*). In such an open system, individuals will feel secure enough to question directly with everyone concerned whether the objective is realistic. In closed systems, the fear of being con-sidered faint-hearted, uninvolved, or unsupportive prevents such doubts being voiced at all. The good leader has an ear to the ground and will know the stage at which real doubts grow. The leader can raise the issue by voicing doubts about the achievability of the goal (*objective*) and can check very quickly whether he or she is trampled underfoot in the rush to agree or scoffed at for their lack of understanding.

2.7 Mentoring, coaching, and team training

From our discussion on team building the project manager clearly has a very important role in fostering a sense of involvement and value – an observation that is completely consistent with research in many different areas of sociology, sociological practice, and psychology, all of which point to the critical importance of the fol-lower and manager relationship. My own personal experience tends to confirm Herzberg's theory that monetary reward is not by itself an incentive. Individuals who work as part of a team require both emotional support and practical help, and the project manager as a leader has the duty to provide both.

Project managers tend to require a high level of situational aware-ness and engagement when it comes to understanding the moti-vational needs of their followers. Returning to our discussion on "motivation" in Section 2.1.1, it is useful to acknowledge the con-tribution made by Douglas McGregor, the inventor of Theory X and Theory Y (see *The Human Side of Enterprise*, 1960). McGregor's Theory X is based on the assumption that a managers role is to coerce and control employees. Theory Y is based on the assumption that a manager's role is to develop the potential in employees and help them to release that potential towards common goals. To this end project managers have a responsibility to ensure that their followers have the opportunity to attain their aspirations (that is their intrinsic desire for personal development and engagement).

2.7.1 Mentoring

Mentoring is about placing the needs of your staff (followers) above your own and ensuring that those needs are met. As Herzberg noted, personnel satisfaction and growth cannot be purchased with money. Nothing challenges people so effectively to improve their self-awareness and performance as a task that places high demands on them. There is a clear link between mentoring and individual development and effectiveness.

The term *mentoring* is defined as: "*an instrument that project managers use to nurture and grow their people. It can be an informal practice or a formal program. The pupil observes, questions, and explores. Mentors demonstrate, explain, and instruct*". To this end the mentor's job is to promote intentional learning, which includes capacity building through methods such as instructing, coaching, providing experiences, modelling, and advising. Mentoring

Table 2.3 Mentoring framework

Personal framework (descriptive view)	Professional framework (descriptive view)
Purpose The mentor is seen as trustworthy and an openness and bond is created	The mentor is seen as a role model and the pupil increases skill and insight
Key activities • Build a strong mentor–pupil relationship • Reinforce pupil's self-esteem and confidence • Explore each others' thoughts, views, and strengths as mentors and as people	• The pupil discovers the world of project management – seeing the "bigger picture" such as: 1. Planning activities and sequence 2. Assessing learning and adjusting instruction 3. Worrying less about following plans and more about accomplishing an objective

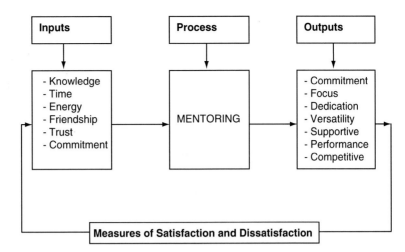

Figure 2.2
High-level view of the mentoring process.

of staff as such is undertaken within a personnel and professional framework; this ensures that the mentoring process is cemented (see Table 2.3 and Figure 2.2).

Project managers do not necessarily make effective mentors; certain individuals are more effective in the role of developing others. Whether or not an individual is suited to the role of mentor may depend on his or her own stage of development and experience. For example, a fairly successful individual may have had a specific or limited background and may not have enough general experience to offer. Prior to entering into a mentoring relationship, the pupil should assume the responsibility of assessing the mentor's potential effectiveness. Although by no means exhaustive, the qualities that are essential in an effective mentor include:

- *A desire to help:* individuals who are interested and willing to help others.
- *Have had positive experiences:* individuals who have had positive formal or informal experiences with a mentor tend to be good mentors themselves.
- *Good reputation for developing others:* experienced people who have a good reputation for helping others develop their skills.
- *Time and energy:* people who have the time and mental energy to devote to the relationship.
- *Useful knowledge:* individuals who have maintained current, up-to-date technological knowledge and/or skills.

- *Learning attitude:* individuals who are still willing and able to learn and who see the potential benefits of a mentoring relationship.
- *Demonstrate mentoring skills*: individuals who have demonstrated effective coaching, counselling, facilitating, and networking skills.

A project manager's time is generally at a premium; so planning ahead for mentoring sessions is a prerequisite. Regular communication is also important in order to effectively maintain the mentor–pupil relationship; not all mentors–pupils will work in the same location. Mentors should record a short summary of their experience with the pupil probably on a quarterly basis. The closer the communication, the more likely the relationship will be successful.

2.7.2 Coaching

Most often we think of coaching as focussing on job performance and on getting people to do things better. This is a part of coaching, but the process of coaching people around their career choices and growth also involves training (see Section 2.7.3). In exploring alternatives, people look around and try out new possibilities for the next stage of their careers. Often, coaching can help here by providing coaches with a person who can help debrief impressions, sort through options, and provide answers to the questions that arise from exploration.

Coaching can be defined as *"a developmental strategy that enables people to meet their goals for improved performance, growth, or career enhancement."* This definition differs from the model that is defined for mentoring. In this definition, the focus is on the "the individual being coached" rather than the coach. The assumption is that the pupil has a goal that the coach (project manager) helps him or her to meet. The relationship involves two-way dialogue rather than one-way narration. Also, the focus is positive and objective on particular improvements that the pupil wants rather than on deficiencies and personality factors. For example, the pupil requires increased knowledge of activity-based planning or testing strategies.

The definition also involves a change in thinking about who can give coaching. While some coaching can be given by the project manager, coaching can be a part of a less formal situation. All that is required is that the coach has the willingness, the insight, the skills, and the perspective that will allow useful insight for the pupil. Coaching should be very flexible and adaptive, and although project managers can be excellent sources of coaching, so too are team members and other colleagues. It should also be pointed out that mentors of any type can often act as coaches. Anyone with the ability and desire to help individuals develop can be a coach.

Exploration should lead to setting developmental goals, which often involve trying out new behaviours. For instance, a technically oriented person such as an architect or a developer, may start taking on managerial and coordination activities as part of a developmental goal around moving into project management. Input and perspective from a coach can be invaluable in making the most out of the learning experiences these activities will involve.

2.7.3 Training

All organizations have an obligation to invest in their people and employees have an obligation to keep their skills up-to-date. The software industry is a dynamic and changing entity. In the past, skills were learned through 5-year apprenticeships or even through the experience of making mistakes. Such an approach today is considered slow and inefficient, especially in software engineering where complexity is a key attribute.

A global software organization employing around 6000 people will invest around £1 billion in training over 25 years. A project manager employed over a 40-year career is expected to earn £1.5 million (McManus, 2005). For many organizations, these two elements represent a significant investment. Although organizations have an obligation to invest in training, they also have a right to see a return on their investment. Managing this people investment within an empowered organization lies in part with the project manager.

Project managers are able to influence outcomes in three ways by:

1. Aligning the training needs of the individual to the mission needs of the project
2. Establishing training priorities that meet skill shortages within the project
3. Targeting training programmes to meet future needs of the project

To this end the project manager needs to know:

- The knowledge capability of the team
- The competencies required for the project(s)
- The competencies required for each position (for example, analyst, developer, architect database designer, etc.)

Table 2.4 Tangible and intangible benefits

Tangible	Intangible
Fewer or lower	
1. Absenteeism	1. Customer complaints
2. Accidents	2. Delays in completing work
3. Equipment breakdowns	3. Employee mistakes
4. Material waste	4. Grievances filed
5. Operating costs	5. Personal conflicts
6. Overtime	6. Policy violations
7. Tardiness	7. Work-related accidents
8. Turnover	
More or improved	
1. Attendance	1. Communication among units
2. Cost reduction	2. Customer satisfaction
3. Goal attainment	3. Employee morale
4. Productivity	4. Employee suggestions
5. Return on invested capital	5. Methods of work
6. Revenue collection	6. Readiness to experiment
7. Units of service (h)	7. Service quality

Training and competency management help focus the organization's efforts to attract and maintain a skilled workforce that is representative of the market diversity, and include the competencies needed to deliver a range of projects and performance that is consistent with the objectives of the business. The challenge for the project manager is in recognizing that no skill or practice will remain in place forever, and the organization must be prepared to continually invest in and improve their training regimes. Table 2.4 lists some of the benefits that might result from an organization's investment in training, some of which are tangible and some intangible.

2.8 Measuring and rewarding team performance

Returning to the discussion of motivation (Section 2.1.1), both Maslow and Herzberg belong to the self-actualizing needs' approach to motivation and each of their models distinguishes between higher and lower order needs. As managers, it is not easy to make predictions about which needs will give rise to a particular form of behaviour, which in turn may be directed towards achieving team and project goals. Needs vary between individuals and each individual's needs will vary over time. Theories proposed by Maslow and Herzberg seek to address the question of "what" motivates people. Alternate theories on motivation (and reward) such as Vroom's Expectancy Theory (VET) concentrate not on what motivates people but "how" they are motivated. This in part is achieved by examining the process, which individuals go through prior to behaving in a given way. Sigmund Freud, for example, believed that all behaviour is motivated by the desire to avoid pain and experience fulfilment. In his view, fulfilment (or satisfaction seeking) is the reason by which anything gets done. We work because it will provide us with things that we think will provide pleasure. While it is obvious that the desire for pleasure is a real and powerful force behind much of what we do it, however, does not explain all behaviour.

Vroom argues that there is a distinct relationship between behaviour, expectation, and reward. VET (Table 2.5) may be viewed as a contingency approach inasmuch that people will act in different ways as they seek differing outcomes and in accordance with their perception of the relationship between performance and outcome. Using Vroom's model, team members (even project managers) will be motivated to behave in certain ways by choosing from a range of outcomes, especially the ones that have the best odds of occurring. For example, if a project team member strongly desires promotion as an outcome (valence), they will perform well if they think that in so doing, there is a high probability that the project manager will actually reward with promotion (expectancy).

Table 2.5 Vroom's expectancy theory

Valence (V) This is the preference an individual has for a particular outcome. It is the individual's perception of the satisfaction they will gain if they achieve the particular outcome

Expectancy (E) This is a subjective probability measure that doing something will actually lead to a particular outcome

Force (F) This is another term for motivation resulting from the interaction of valances for various possible outcomes and the expectancy that action will lead to those outcomes

Relationship (M) The relationship between these factors is given in the following equation:

Motivation $F = fS(E \times V)$,

where

V is the expectancy that action will be followed by desired outcome

E is the strength of preference for a particular outcome, and

S is the summation, included since a particular course of action typically has more than one outcome

---

Using the information outlined in Table 2.4, the motivational force of a job or task can therefore be calculated if the expectancy, instrumentality, and valence values are known. The individual's abilities, traits, role perceptions, and opportunities attenuate the motivational force.

The main contribution of this theory has been to highlight the effects of cognitive and perceptual processes on objective work conditions. It suggests that project managers need to pay attention to four main aspects of their subordinate's perceptions:

1. Project managers should focus on the crucial expectancy values (the link between effort and their performance).
2. Project managers should determine what outcome an employee values.
3. Project managers need to link the reward that subordinates value to their performance.
4. Project managers need to ensure that wage rates are not perceived as inequitable.

2.8.1 Performance setting within projects

In software projects, the actual work of task execution gets done in the producing or implementation phases of the project. In these phases, the focus is on efficiency in satisfying the customer(s) needs under time, cost, and quality project constraints. This is achieved through effective performance setting and communication, the essential basis for project control. Therefore, the key to success here is through establishing performance criteria and efficient management of performance criterion.

Performance criterion should be built around connecting and reinforcing measures derived from the organization's project and customer strategy. Measures should tie directly to customer and stakeholder value and to overall performance. The use of measures should therefore channel different activities in consistent directions. Measures thereby need to serve both as a communications tool and a basis for deploying consistent overall performance requirements. Such alignment ensures consistency of purpose while also supporting innovation and decision making (see Figure 2.3).

Alignment as Andrew Dillane, IT director at CNC Global, puts it is to ensure, *"There is a direct relationship between morale and an individual's ability to contribute."* So make sure all members of your IT

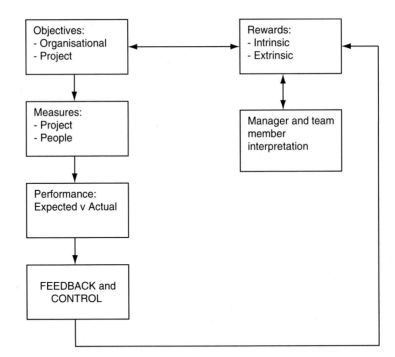

Figure 2.3
Relationships
between objectives,
measures, and
rewards.

staff get to sink their teeth into the projects that bring the most value to the enterprise. Soon after he became CIO of The Huntington National Bank in March 2001, Joe Gottron and his team worked closely with the business units and the finance department to replace an ineffective "all you could ask for" work-request system and a "who you knew" prioritization system with a chargeback process for application development and project management. This new process has dramatically improved productivity and morale. *"The new process provides interconnectivity between projects, budgets, and resources,"* says Gottron. "Today, business unit priorities are very clear, and the technology team knows that what they're working on truly matters to the business. That creates a great deal of energy and motivation."

(*Source: Martha Heller, Six ways to boost morale, CIO 2003*)

A major consideration in setting performance criterion involves the selection and use of performance measures (or metrics). The measures selected should best represent the factors that lead to improved customer, operational, and financial performance. A comprehensive set of measures or indicators tied to customer, stakeholder, and/or organizational performance requirements represents a clear basis for aligning all projects with your organization's goals. Through the analysis of data from your tracking processes, your measures or indicators themselves may be evaluated and changed to better support your project and business goals.

Although by no means exhaustive, measures and indicators of project performance might include:

- Changes resulting from innovations in delivery
- Use of technology
- Effectiveness and direction of resources
- Effectiveness of development methods
- Effectiveness of services
- Improved performance of administrative and other support functions
- Improvement in safety
- Significant innovations in services or technology.

2.8.1.1 People measures

Unlike those project measures stated earlier, people measures attempt to quantify or characterize the behavioural attributes of people, which by their very nature do not lend themselves to easy quantification. That is why there are not as many project people metrics as there are project metrics. Project people metrics are intended to assess, directly or indirectly, whether the team members execute their tasks effectively. Project people metrics are indicators of existence of procedures for conflict management, communication, collaboration, teamwork, and technical competency. The people metrics also deal with the features of the environment that promote leadership, integrity, and professional responsibility. Thus, project people metrics can be viewed as metrics that measure the friendliness of organization towards the project team and the team towards itself.

Although by no means exhaustive, project people performance measures might include:

- Number of ideas generated and implemented
- Number of hours spent mentoring other team members
- Number of hours spent on training (training vs learning outcomes)
- Number of hours spent in meetings
- Number of hours billed to the project
- Number of hours spent on task or job rotation
- Number of hours lost due to sickness
- Number of behavioural issues recorded or resolved

Despite a wealth of research highlighting the positive motivational benefits of performance-related measures, many organizations and their project managers still provide individuals with little or no information about their performance. Although feedback can have considerable impact on both motivation and learning, implementing feedback performance programmes can have wider implications. Feedback can affect the relationship between individual team members and project managers by disrupting existing authority structures. Guirdham (1995) suggests that an effective feedback needs to be:

1. *Generally positive:* reward is more effective than punishment.
2. *Well timed:* as soon as possible.
3. *Control:* the feedback should be about behaviour the individual has control over.
4. *Specific:* feedback should not be general.
5. *Publicly observed:* should not based on revelations or secrets.
6. *Sensitive:* so that it does not trigger the individual's defence mechanisms.

Project team members and other stakeholders should be made aware of the long-term benefits of performance management programme, and the obstacles that would exist during the implementation of the metrics programme. In order to facilitate the programme's successful implementation, communication about the performance initiatives must be direct, consistent, and widespread. Every effort should be made such that the implementation of the programme does not become an organizational secret, because that will only breed notions of conspiracy. Each person's involvement and expectation in the programme should be known and communicated. Ongoing training may be necessary to keep the programme in focus and on track. Implementing a performance management programme requires a cultural change in the organization. The project manager or whoever is responsible for the programme should have strong communication skills and must balance the metrics programme's needs with the participant's readiness to accept and embrace it.

2.8.2 Rewarding performance

As already discussed, there is a strong correlation between motivation, expectation, performance, reward, and sustainable project success. Performance measures work when they are created for the right reasons, and in the right way. The critical decision for any project manager or leader who wants to get higher performance from an individual or group of people is determining whether the group should work as a team, or whether they should be satisfied with what may be termed a single unit. Single units are intrinsically faster and more efficient than teams. Tasks are more clearly defined by one leader, and members work on their own much of the time, enabling individuals to take responsibility for their own actions and enabling the project manager to measure and reward performance in a more direct manner.

None of the motivational approaches discussed so far can be divorced from the organizational culture and the issues associated with rewards and performance should be considered in the context of the culture in which the organization operates. With this point made, three headings are used to further explore the elements and mechanics of reward-based systems.

1. Performance appraisal systems

Performance appraisal systems operate on many levels; the question here is whether the method supports or hinders the motivational strategy of the organization. In my experience, few organizations or their employees are ever completely satisfied with their reward systems. For the project manager, it is important that individuals are appraised on results and behaviour that the organization (and the manager) wants to achieve.

2. Incentive systems

Appraisal systems are generally linked to incentive systems (of some description), but not all incentive systems are linked to appraisal. A bonus system for coding work is unlikely to have any link with personal appraisal while the merit increase of a project manager may be entirely based on the results of a performance review. Incentive covers a number of different attributes:

- Not all incentives are pay related.
- Performance-related pay schemes set out to reward effort in a way that reflects the economic value of that effort.
- Concerns about pay are not always about absolute values but about feeling whether they are fair in relation to what others get.
- An existing incentive scheme may be difficult to change but may have to change to reflect the operating conditions of the organization.

3. Pay and benefits systems

Pay and benefits systems are increasingly finding favour with many larger organizations. These type systems, sometimes referred to as total remuneration systems, incorporate both the intrinsic and extrinsic elements of reward. These systems are generally applied to all employees at all levels of the organization. Such systems include:

- Basic salary
- Bonuses
- Share options
- Child care
- Sick pay
- Discount facilities
- Lunch vouchers
- Tickets to sporting events
- Additional training
- Payment of professional fees
- Free car parking
- Special award dinners
- Outings to the theatre
- Leisure facilities

2.8.3 Maintaining momentum (a question of balance)

The problems associated with not clearly determining the primary purpose of a performance measurement programme are often apparent with organization-wide performance measurement programmes. These programmes tend to be implemented by central Human Resources (HR) departments, whose principal focus is on the development and execution of the organization's assets. This is generally a policy process, and as such, tends to be highly politicized and visible. Project management and operational-level performance improvements are rarely a significant issue in this context. HR policy makers instead are far more interested in how resource allocations support (or do not support) a preferred strategic orientation regarding the role of project management in their jurisdiction. Unfortunately, one-size-fits-all performance measurement programmes that attempt to support both policy-making and project delivery produce voluminous amounts of relatively useless information that effectively support neither policy making nor project delivery. A more useful approach is to clearly and explicitly define, prior to developing a performance measurement programme and collecting any performance information:

- The primary users and beneficiaries of the programme
- The information they need (see Table 2.6)

Table 2.6 Attributes of a performance measurement programme

Performance measurement	Definition	Example
Performance targets	Performance targets are commitments to attain certain programme results in a specified time	In 2006, we aim to reduce coding errors by 20%. This will free up 10,000 h of productive time
Performance measures	Performance measures are the observable factors that are measured over time Hours spent in rectifying coding errors	Number of coding errors per developer; money (in pounds) expended on coding corrections
Performance reporting	A verbal or written communication to employees on the achievements against targets	Weekly progress report Monthly highlight report Quarterly management report
Performance reward	The tangible and intangible returns to employees for the results achieved	Bonuses Merit payments Client satisfaction Employee recognition Increased training

- How they intend to use the information for decision making and/or project delivery
- How the information should be communicated to users and how to handle negative information

With these clarifications in hand, a more useful measurement programme can be constructed that meets its users' specific information needs. The programme should then be regularly monitored, analysed, and improved so that it continues to add value to its users' decision-making and project-delivery efforts. If a performance measurement programme fails at this task, one could reasonably ask, "What is the point in having one?"

2.9 Chapter summary – 10 key points

The most important points to take away from this chapter are:

1. A project manager has an obligation to sow the seeds of success.

2. A project manager's self-disclosure fosters trust as it leads to shared perceptions and concerns.

3. In creating high-performance project teams, it is not enough for the project manager to act as the person who sets goals and enforces certain standards of behaviour.

4. The rationale for empowerment approaches in project management is very compelling and arises from an increasing recognition that project managers do not hold a monopoly on technical knowledge or wisdom and to sustain satisfaction and motivation; there needs to be a greater role for the team followers in the social, economic, and political spheres that shape the project and their careers.

5. Whilst the absence of these motivators will not necessarily cause team members to resign, an increase in their strength will lead directly to increased individual fulfilment. In turn, this will lead to sustained or higher levels of performance.

6. In project management, the single and most important constraint is "time" and time places demands on managers and team members alike and because time is at a premium, it is the measure by which many objectives are measured.

7. Project managers tend to require a high level of situational awareness and engagement when it comes understanding the motivational needs of their followers.

8. Project managers do not necessarily make effective mentors; certain individuals are more effective in the role of developing others.

9. Project team members and other stakeholders should be made aware of the long-term benefits of performance management programme, and the obstacles that would exist during the implementation of the metrics programme.

10. There is a strong correlation between motivation, expectation, performance, reward, and sustainable project success. Performance measures work when they are created for the right reasons, and when they are created in the right way.

2.10 Next chapter

In the next chapter, we will explore some of the concepts, ideas, and issues associated with decision making and problem solving in project management. We will also explore some decision-making strategies and the tools used in decision making.

Chapter references

Guirdham, M. (1995) Interpersonal Skills at Work (2nd edition), Hemel Hempstead, Prentice Hall.

Harvey-Jones, J. (1988) Making IT Happen: Reflections on Leadership, UK, Collins Publication.

Hayes, K. (2000) A Practical Guide to Leadership Coaching, The Learning Attitude Ltd.

McGregor, D. (1960) The Human Side of Enterprise, New York, McGraw-Hill.

McManus, J. (2005) The cost of training, Research paper based on Computer Weekly Archive Material (unpublished).

Page, N. and E. Czuba (1999) Empowerment: what is it? Journal of Extension, 37(5).

Thomas, K. and B. Velthouse (1990) Cognitive elements of empowerment: An "interpretive" model of intrinsic task motivation. Academy of Management Review, 15, 666–681.

Further reading

Bennis, W. (1997) Organising Genius: The Secrets of Creative Collaboration, Reading, MA, Addison Wesley.

Deci, E. and R. Ryan (1985) The support of autonomy and control of behavior. Journal of Personality and Social Psychology, 53, 1024–1037.

McManus, J. and T. Wood-Harper (2003) Information Systems Project Management: Methods, Tools and Techniques, Upper Saddle River, NJ, Pearson Education (Prentice Hall).

Wellins, R.S. et al. (1991) Empowered Teams, San Francisco, CA, Jossey–Bass Publishers.

Vroom, V.H. (1964) Work and Motivation, New York, Wiley Publication.

Leadership and Decision Making

3.1 The decision-making process

Returning to our discussion on ACL in Chapter 1 (Section 1.4.1), Professor Adair argues that to achieve an objective (or task), or lead and guide a team in the right direction, a leader needs the ability to think and make decisions. Making decisions is ultimately what project managers (and many leaders) are paid for. According to Drucker, the first managerial skill is the making of effective decisions. Project managers make decisions every day, most of the decisions made will be routine and low risk. However, every decision, no matter how small, requires an assessment of objectives, alternatives, and potential risks.

Almost 20 years of my life was spent working in the software industry, and experience has taught me that complex projects usually demand a high level of technical skill, intellect, and a reasonable degree of intervention by the project manager. Contemporary research supports the notion that many projects fail because not enough attention is paid to the technical and stakeholder aspects of project delivery. Many of the causes of failed projects can be traced back to poor leadership and poor decision making.

Making decisions is by and large what project managers do. How well (or effectively) they make such decisions will be based on the criteria of behavioural history, situational beliefs, personal values, social and occupational norms, personality, and environmental constraints. Project managers make decisions every day. In making decisions, the project manager must resolve the following important questions:

- What decision needs to be made?
- When does it have to be made?
- Who will decide?

- Who will need to be consulted?
- Who will ratify or veto the decision?
- Who will need to be informed of the decision?

Answering these questions is sometimes difficult even for seasoned project managers. Clearly each decision must have an outcome that is context specific. In many situations, a decision maker's outcome does not depend on his or her own choice alone but upon the choices of others (McManus and Wood-Harper, 2003).

An assumption underlying the study of leadership is that leaders affect organizational performance through the decisions they make. Decisions made by project managers can be divided into two types. The first decision type is made as we respond to a developing problem or crisis, which can either be technical (a software problem, for example) or involve people (for example, moving the team to a different geographical location). The second type is the forward-programmed (or forward-looking) decision, which tends to be strategic in nature. For example, do we invest in a new type of software technology or programming language? Key attributes in the decision situation to be assessed are shown in Figure 3.1.

3.1.1 A framework for decision making

Many methods and techniques have been proposed to assist the manager in decision evaluation; however, the framework offered by Herbert Simon is favoured because it supports many of the characteristics and practices that managers associate with making decisions in the commercial and technical world of project management where the mitigation of risk is seen by senior management as a prerequisite to successful project delivery. In Herbert Simon's view, decision making involves intelligence, design, choice, and implementation (Simon, 1977). This decision evaluation framework developed by Simon is divided into four stages. In brief, there is recognition of a decision need or opportunity, and the identification of possible causes, the development of alternative solutions, the selection among alternative causes of actions, and carrying out the chosen action. These stages are also reflected in the model of Adair where they are termed as define objectives, collect information, develop options, evaluate, and implement. For the purpose of discussion, the four-stage framework suggested by Simon will be used as a proxy for general discussion.

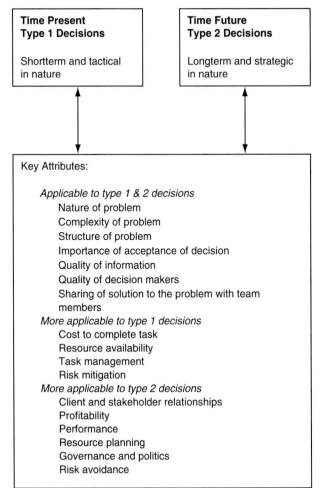

Figure 3.1
Decision-making
profiles.

1. Perception of decision need or opportunity

It is evident that decision making is dependent on how well the facts and issues facing the project, business, or customer are understood. Before a decision can be made, the problem must first be perceived and understood. This process is referred to as framing. Beach (1990) for example, discerns three distinct but related images that decision makers use for framing. Together they form the cognitive structure of the decision maker. They are:

● The value image, consisting of the decision maker's principles like values, moral standards, beliefs, ethics, etc.

- The trajectory image, consisting of the decision maker's agenda for the future (both personal and for the organization), the decision maker's objectives, and timelines.
- The strategic image, consisting of the decision maker's plans to accomplish the particular objectives, as well as the decision maker's projections of the effects of implementing the plans in terms of the chances of successfully attaining the goals.

During this initial stage, Simon differentiates between what he calls "programmed and unprogrammed" decisions: the first being those capable of processing to an established pattern, the second embracing new or complex situations for which there may be no precedent. In my experience, project managers tend to encounter the latter type of situation most often.

2. Formulation of alternative courses of action

This is perhaps the most critical stage within the entire process. During this stage, it is essential that the individual decision makers (and other participants) pay attention to the impact interdependencies brought to bear on the decision-making process. For example, a major characteristic of software projects is that, in general, they involve many interdependencies and many more uncertainties than technologists like to admit.

In formulating alternative courses of action, it is not unusual to engage the efforts of individual members of the project team or supporting stakeholders. This approach usually ensures that a broad range of opinions are taken into account and allows individuals to test out their ideas. During this process the project manager should not side with any one individual or idea; in essence, this is a meeting of minds (rational or otherwise).

Paradoxically, due to many cognitive limitations, individual decision makers tend to reflect a number of characteristics that may have a negative impact on the process. Harrison (1987) provides an overview of these characteristics:

- Human subjects tend to overestimate low probabilities of events and underestimate high probabilities.
- Individuals appear to be insensitive to the sample size of their observations.
- Individuals adjust their first approximations to an estimate on the basis of additional evidence.
- Individuals tend to be overconfident of their ability to estimate the probability of an uncertain event.

- Individuals tend to overestimate the probability of events that actually occur, as well as the extent to which they or others would have been able to predict past events.
- Human subjects reveal a tendency to compare pairs of alternatives rather than a whole list.
- Individuals tend to minimize reliance on explicit trade-offs or other numerical computations.
- Individuals exhibit choices that are sometimes inconsistent and intransitive.

Prior to commencing this stage it is good practice to ensure that all those involved in the decision-making process are conversant with the task objective, principles, policies, and rules of conduct.

3. Evaluation of alternatives for their respective contributions

Although the Simon decision evaluation framework was chosen here regardless of the model used by the decision maker in selecting the best alternative, some characteristics of the decision maker and of the decision task itself influence the decision. With regard to the decision task, the following characteristics are pertinent:

- *Unfamiliarity:* the degree to which the decision task is foreign to the decision maker.
- *Ambiguity:* the degree to which the decision task is unclear to the decision maker.
- *Complexity:* the number of different components of the decision task—the number of alternatives to be considered, the amount of relative information to be considered, and the number of criteria applied.
- *Instability:* the degree to which objectives, criteria, and constraints change during decision making.
- *Reversibility:* the degree to which the choice can be reversed if necessary.
- *Significance:* the importance of the decision to the decision maker and the organization.
- *Accountability:* the degree to which the decision maker is accountable for the consequences of the decision.
- *Time and/or money constraints:* the limitations on time and money during the decision-making process.

During the evaluation process, it is highly likely that the evaluators will use both qualitative and quantitative tools in the evaluation process. Evaluating information and data can be a time-consuming process. The use of decision-support tools (DST) can assist the decision maker and save time in data evaluation. As an example, DST can undertake "what if analysis" or produce prespecified reports for project managers on an exception basis. DST ought to help project managers to select a proper course of action and then provide feedback on the success of the implemented decision. Of course, this assumes that enough information was gathered during stage 1 and a sufficient number of alternatives were evaluated during stage 2. If not, the project manager may choose to return to either of these stages for more data or to examine alternative courses of action.

4. *Choice of one or more alternatives for implementation*

The basis for choosing a particular way for implementing a decision is not governed merely by considerations of conventional logic or rationality. Decisions are also likely to involve considerations of justice and fairness as perceived by various stakeholders and by considerations of personal ethics or morality as perceived by different persons. In essence, the decision adopted should always be amongst the legitimate alternatives considered, that is, it should represent a course of action that is satisfactory to all concerned. Sometimes, this may mean that we demand more of team members and stakeholders than they are capable of giving. In these cases, people must be mentored or coached to contribute more; leadership is clearly a contributory factor in this process.

To sum up this section, in the world of project management any decision made by an individual or group must be implemented by an individual manager who is personally responsible for the outcome of their actions. It is prudent to remember that responsible managers do not hold a group responsible for its choice. Responsibility lies with the individual manager.

3.1.2 Some limitations

The most important resource whose limitations have to be considered is people who carry out the decision. No decision can be better than the people who have to carry it out. Their vision, competence, skill, and understanding determine what they can and cannot do. Going back to the Harrison list of characteristics, the wrong decision must never be adopted because people and the competence to do what is right are lacking. Decisions should always lie between genuine alternatives, that is, between courses of action every one of which will adequately solve the problem.

It is acknowledged, however, that decisions and resulting judgements sometimes come down to a single issue. It has been noted that, given the resource constraints, most decision makers will choose to satisfy rather than optimize when faced with a decision situation.

Ironically managers being human beings will rarely act as rational beings that insist that all relevant information be gathered, all rational alternatives be considered, and only the optimum alternative be chosen. Instead, they will act with bounded rationality, that is, they will be satisfied to make a decision based on incomplete information and a limited number of alternatives, if it meets some of their subjective preferences and produces an acceptable level of results.

Two decades ago, Andrew George offered advice to decision makers who applied bounded rationality to ill-structured problems that rely on multiple points of view. He highlighted when and where potential problems may occur. These include:

- When the decision maker and his or her advisors agree too readily on the nature of the problem facing them and on a response to it.
- When advisors and policy advocates take different positions and debate them before the executive, but their disagreements do not cover the full range of relevant hypotheses and alternative options.
- When there is no advocate for an unpopular policy option.
- When advisors to the executive thrash out their disagreements over policy without the executive's knowledge and confront him or her with a unanimous recommendation.
- When advisors agree privately among themselves that the executive ought to face up to a difficult decision, but no one is willing to alert him or her to the need to do so.
- When the executive, faced with an important decision, is dependent on a single channel of information.
- When the key assumptions and premises of a plan that the executive is asked to adopt have been evaluated only by advocates of that option.
- When the executive asks advisors for their opinions on a preferred course of action but does not request a qualified group to examine more carefully the negative judgement offered by one or more advisors.

- When the executive is impressed by the consensus among team advisors on behalf of a particular option but fails to ascertain how firm the consensus is, how it was achieved, and whether it is justified.

3.2 Decision-making tools and techniques

In Section 3.1 it was noted that decision makers may use a range of qualitative and quantitative tools and techniques to assist them in evaluating and formulating their decision-making strategies. In principle, qualitative and quantitative tools and techniques are just a means to an end, not an end, in themselves. Decision making, as Drucker states, is not always a mechanical job. It is risk taking and a challenge to judgement. Without being repetitious, the importance of decision making in project management is generally recognized. However, a great deal of the discussion tends to focus on problem solving, that is, on giving answers. And that is the wrong focal point. The most common source of mistakes in management decisions is the emphasis on finding the right answer rather than the right question (Drucker, 1954).

The only decisions that are really important are the type 2 decisions (Figure 3.1). They involve either finding out what the situation is or changing it, or what the resources are or what they should be. These are specifically project management decisions. Any project manager has to make such strategic decisions, and the higher "your" level in the hierarchy, the more you must make.

Depending on the tools and techniques used, decision making can either be time wasting or the project manager's best means of finding the right question and the answers to it. Although good decision making is aided by the use of tools and techniques, it also depends heavily on experience and judgement. There are over 100 decision-making tools and techniques available to the project manager. I have selected 10 examples, of which five are qualitative and five quantitative tools and techniques that cover three broad decision areas: prioritizing, cost–benefit, and optimization.

3.2.1 Tools and techniques

3.2.1.1 Qualitative tools and techniques

1. *Brainstorming:* the term is commonly used for creative thinking. The basis of brainstorming is generating ideas in a group

situation, based on the principle of suspending judgement – a principle, which scientific research has proved to be highly productive in individual as well as group effort. The process includes:

- Arranging a meeting for a group of the right size and makeup (typically 4–6 people).
- Writing the initial topic on a flip board, whiteboard, or other system where everyone can see it. The better defined and more clearly stated the problem, the better the session tends to be.
- Making sure that everyone understands the problem or issue. Review the ground rules.
- Having someone facilitate to enforce the rules and write down all the ideas as they occur (the scribe can be a second person).
- Generating ideas – either in an unstructured (anyone can articulate an idea at any time) or structured way (going round the table, allowing people to pass if they have no new ideas).
- Clarifying and concluding the session. Ideas that are identical can be combined; all others should be kept separate. It is useful to get a consensus of which ideas should be looked at further, or what the next action and timescale is.

Despite some limitations, brainstorming remains a popular technique. For many groups, it has provided a first clear picture of their potential to think creatively together and to move off in new directions. It also lets everyone know where the ideas have come from, thus setting the stage for consensus and action. Since brainstorming is an expansive, divergent thinking approach that generates lots of ideas, it needs to be followed by a narrowing, focussing activity that extracts a reasonable number of promising ideas for the group to work with.

2. *Brain writing (6–3–5)*: each person, using Post-it notes or small cards, writes down ideas and places them in the centre of the table. Everyone is free to pull out one or more of these ideas for inspiration. Team members can create new ideas and variations or piggyback on existing ideas. The term *brain writing (6–3–5)* comes from the process of having six people write three ideas in 5 min. Each person has a blank 6–3–5 worksheet. Everyone writes the problem statement at the top of his or her worksheet (word-for-word from an agreed problem definition). They then write three ideas on the top row of the worksheet in 5 min in a complete and concise sentence

(6–10 words). At the end of 5 min (or when everyone has finished writing) the worksheet is passed to the person on right. This person now adds three more ideas. The process continues until the worksheet is completed. There will now be a total of 108 ideas on the six worksheets. These can now be assessed.

3. *Card story board:* this technique although similarly named is quite different from the picture story board technique. It is an "idea"-organizing method using tree logic and other hierarchical diagrams and outlines. In essence, cards are laid out in a tabular format – a simple row of header cards (or possibly header and subheader cards), each with a column of idea cards below it, perhaps with added action or comment notes attached (index cards or Post-it slips could be used). The process is as follows:

   - The group leader describes the problem to the participants; they then suggest possible categories of solutions. These are written on cards and displayed as a row of "headers".
   - The group leader selects a particular "header" and participants write ideas relating to that header on cards. These idea cards are displayed under the relevant header, followed by the leader posing provocative questions to prompt further idea-cards under that header. This process is repeated with other headers, until there is an adequate supply of ideas. If necessary, Step 1 is returned back to generate further headers, or add subheader cards, or both under a particular header card.
   - The idea cards should now be ranked via a suitable voting method and arranged in priority order under each header (or subheader). The best three in each category are discussed further, and ranked amongst themselves.

4. *Consensus mapping:* consensus mapping helps a facilitator and group reach consensus about how best to arrange a network of up to maybe 20 activities that have to be sequenced over time into a useable plan of action (for example, replacing a legacy system with new integrated IT systems). These will usually be activities that could be done in a range of orders. The order has to be approved; it is not given by the internal logic of the activities themselves. The technique has parallels to many of the usual project-planning methods (and could if necessary feed into them) but operates at a purely qualitative, outline level.

5. *Dimensional analysis:* the dimensional-analysis technique is a checklist that relates to five Ws and H and is of most use as an aide memoir for initial exploration of a problem or evaluating options, particularly those associated with human relations rather than those of a technical nature. Jensen (1978) defines a problem that is reflected in:

- Spatial dimension (Where?): refers to distribution of items space. For example, the classification of annual sales by geographical area would be a spatial classification.
- Temporal (When?): refers to the time at which the subject matter in question occurred. For example, the analysis of annual sales by weeks, months, and quarters would be a temporal classification.
- Quantitative (How much?): the basis of distinction rests upon differences in quantity. For example, the analysis sales according to differences in volume (m^3) or value (£) would be a quantitative classification.
- Qualitative (How serious): involves the necessity to distinguish between differences in quality or condition. For example, an analysis of sales by product group involves qualitative distinctions.

3.2.1.2 Quantitative decision tools and techniques

1. *Analytical hierarchy process (AHP):* This is a quantitative comparison method used to select a preferred alternative by using pairwise comparisons of the alternatives based on their relative performance against the criteria. The basis of this technique is that humans are more capable of making relative judgements than absolute judgements. The AHP is a systematic procedure for representing the elements of any problem, hierarchically. It organizes the basic rationality by breaking down a problem into its smaller and smaller constituent parts and then guides decision makers through a series of pairwise comparison judgements (which are documented and can be re-examined) to express the relative strength or intensity of impact of the elements and the hierarchy. These judgements are then translated to numbers (ratio–scale estimates). The AHP includes procedures and principles used to synthesize many judgements to derive priorities among criteria and subsequently for alternative solutions. Alternatives and criteria are scored using a pairwise comparison method and mathematics. The pairwise comparisons are made using a nine-point scale:

1 = Equal importance or preference
3 = Moderate importance or preference of one over another
5 = Strong or essential importance or preference
7 = Very strong or demonstrated importance or preference
9 = Extreme importance or preference.

The calculations are easily set up in a spreadsheet and commercial software packages are available.

2. *Cost–benefit analysis (CBA):* CBA is "a systematic quantitative method of assessing the desirability of government projects or policies when it is important to take a long view of future effects and a broad view of possible side effects". It is a good approach when the primary basis for making decisions is the monetary cost versus the monetary benefit of the alternatives. The standard criterion for deciding whether a project can be justified on economic principles is net present value – the discounted monetized value of expected net benefits (i.e. benefits minus costs). Net present value is computed by assigning monetary values to benefits and costs, discounting future benefits and costs using an appropriate discount rate, and subtracting the sum total of discounted costs from the sum total of discounted benefits. Discounting benefits and costs transforms gains and losses occurring in different time periods to a common unit of measurement. Projects with positive net present value increase social resources and are generally preferred. Projects with negative net present value should generally be avoided. When "benefits" and "costs" can be quantified in terms of sterling pounds (as, for example, avoided cost) over several years, these benefits can be subtracted from the costs (or outlays) and the present value of the benefit calculated. "Both intangible and tangible benefits and costs should be recognized. Costs should reflect opportunity cost of any resources used, measured by the return to those resources in their most productive application elsewhere." The alternative returning the largest discounted benefit is preferred. In pros and cons analysis, cost is regarded intuitively along with the other advantages and disadvantages ("low cost" is a pro; "high cost" is a con). The other techniques provide numerical ranking of alternatives based on either intangible or tangible benefits.

3. *Kepner and Tregoe decision analysis:* It is a quantitative comparison method in which a team of experts numerically score criteria and alternatives based on individual judgements or assessments. The size of the team needed tends to be inversely

proportional to the quality of the data available – the more intangible and qualitative the data, the greater the number of people that should be involved. In KTDA parlance, each evaluation criterion is first scored based on its relative importance to the other criteria (1 = least; 10 = most). These scores become the criteria weights. "Once the WANT objectives (goals) have been identified, each one is weighted according to its relative importance. The most important objective is identified and given a weight of 10. All other objectives are then weighted in comparison with the first, from 10 (equally important) down to a possible 1 (not very important). When the time comes to evaluate the alternatives, we do so by assessing them relative to each other against all WANT objectives – one at a time."

The alternatives are scored individually against each of the goal criteria based on their relative performance. We give a score of 10 to the alternative that comes closest to meeting the objective, and score the other alternatives relative to it. It is not an ideal that we seek through this comparative evaluation. What we seek is an answer to the question "of these (real and attainable) alternatives, which best fulfils the objective?" A total score is determined for each alternative by multiplying its score for each criterion by the criterion weights (relative weighting factor for each criterion) and then summing across all criteria. The preferred alternative will have the highest total score.

KTDA is suitable for moderately complex decisions involving a few criteria. The method requires only basic arithmetic. Its main disadvantage is that it may not be clear how much better a score of "10" is than a score of "8," for example. Moreover, total alternative scores may be close together, making a clear choice difficult.

4. *Multiattribute utility theory (MAUT):* This is a quantitative comparison method used to combine dissimilar measures of costs, risks, and benefits, along with individual and stakeholder preferences, into high-level, aggregated preferences. The foundation of MAUT is the use of utility functions. Utility functions transform diverse criteria to one common, dimensionless scale (0–1) known as the multiattribute "utility". Once utility functions are created an alternative's raw data (objective) or the analyst's beliefs (subjective) can be converted to utility scores. As with the other methods, the criteria are weighted according to importance. To identify the

preferred alternative, multiply each normalized alternative's utility score results for all of an alternative's criteria. The preferred alternative will have the highest total score. Utility functions (and MAUT) are typically used, when quantitative information is known about each alternative, which can result in firmer estimates of the alternative performance. Utility graphs are created based on the data for each criterion. Every decision criterion has a utility function created for it. The utility functions transform an alternative's raw score to a dimensionless utility score, between 0 and 1. The utility scores are weighted by multiplying the utility score by the weight of the decision criterion – which reflects the decision-making support staff's and decision maker's values – and totalled for each alternative. The total scores indicate the ranking of the alternatives. The MAUT evaluation method is suitable for complex decisions with multiple criteria and many alternatives. Additional alternatives can be readily added to a MAUT analysis, provided they have data available to determine the utility from the utility graphs. Once the utility functions have been developed, any number of alternatives can be scored against them.

5. *Mathematical programming:* The procedures adopted in mathematical programming follow those experiences the decision maker uses in practice. When a decision maker is confronted with a problem that has many interlocking aspects, an initial solution to the problem might be to meet the minimum requirements, regardless of the cost. Various changes to this initial solution could then be introduced one at a time, in an effort to improve the current solution. A mathematical programming model has two major parts: the objective function and the constraints. The basic types of mathematical programming models are: linear, nonlinear, and integer programming.

3.3 Decision-making strategies

Decision makers formulate strategies while decision-making strategies involve the interpersonal skills used for a group to reach a decision. How a project manager and the team reach an agreement and commit to the agreement requires serious effort for most people. The common approach for project teams is to elect or appoint a leader (not always the project manager) who will try to guide the team's discussions to reach team agreement. As discussed in Section 2.1, many teams shun this traditional model as potentially manipulative and detrimental to the building of trust that is so necessary for strengthening teams. Since many individuals in the West come from democratic roots, it is natural for a team to want to set a standard of unanimous agreement – an ideal state that is difficult and sometimes impossible to achieve. Often the seemingly simple prospect of getting the whole team to agree to the time and place of the next project meeting can turn out to be an imposing task.

The way in which decisions are made in any project or group depends on the power structure and nature of the group leadership. The way in which a decision has been reached can have a profound affect on our confidence and trust. (For example, was I listened to? Was I heard? Was I even invited to contribute? Does my opinion carry weight or can I easily be ignored? Trust for the individual is an integral part of team development.) The effect of decisions on our careers and on the careers of others also affects our growth and the growth of our team members. Who is chiefly responsible for making decisions? What process is used to make them? What part do you play in the decision making? We are much more committed to carrying out decisions that we have helped to make. If we have little input, we will have little interest in what happens. But if we are involved in planning or in consultation, we will have a real stake in the outcome.

Some decision-making strategies involve only the project manager or a few persons in a somewhat unilateral mode, while others involve the entire team through discussion. There are four ways in which decisions are normally made. These are:

1. Authoritarian
2. Subgroup
3. Majority
4. Consensus

1. Authoritarian

Project managers who are task driven tend to be characterized as being strong, competent, and dominant. Their management and leadership style tends to be autocratic and their relationship with subordinates is mainly directional, in that it involves the issuing of orders. Project managers who adopt (or have) this type of style tend to make quick decisions and those decisions are assumed to be final. On the surface, this is efficient and time-saving process. But it often leads to disagreement and resentment. If discussion and questioning are forbidden, misinterpretation of the decision may be widespread.

2. Subgroup

Subgroup decision making involves a small part of the team or the total group. They gain sufficient influence to force the project manager or leader or the group to adopt a decision. An example of this is in health-related projects, when a small minority of clinical consultants insists on certain Clinical and Governance rights and the majority goes along with that decision. The subgroup method can be effective if the subgroup approaches the task to assist the full team, and if the team requested the subgroup to work as such.

3. Majority

The majority-decision process does not require consensus for group action. Instead, decisions are made by voting with a majority determining the position of the entire group. This approach has the advantage of being able to produce a prompt and clear decision. (It may take some time before consensus processes can reach a decisions – if they can at all.) Unfortunately, majority rule processes provide only limited incentives for the participants to compromise or to find a way for dealing with issues that serve the interests of all participants. Instead, the incentive is to compromise only enough to build a majority coalition. A specific weakness of majority decision making is that some percentage of the group, sometimes as much as 49%, may disagree with the outcome. This means that almost half the group may be unhappy over a decision. Once a winning coalition has been achieved, the majority are largely free to ignore the interests of other participants.

4. Consensus decision making

In contrast to authoritarian and subgroup decision process, consensus decision making is a powerful tool for bringing groups together to move forward with decisions that are inspired and effective. However, like many tools, using consensus requires learning a particular set of skills. Groups who try to apply it without learning those skills often end up frustrated, when what is really needed is more training, knowledge, and practice. Cooperation is the basis of community. Consensus is a thoroughly cooperative form of decision making. While not appropriate for all situations, it is not generally recommended for a quick fix to a crisis. For groups that have a shared purpose, explicit values, some level of trust and openness to each other, and enough time to work with material in depth, the consensus process can be immensely rewarding. In contrast with the separations of majority voting, consensus bonds people together. The search for consensus agreement relies on every person in the team bringing their best self-forward to seek unity. The group need not all think the same, have the same opinion, or support the same proposal in a unanimous vote. Rather, what is being earnestly sought is a sense of the meeting. This is the essence of what the group agrees on, the common ground, the shared understanding or desire. If a team member cannot live with the decision, you do not have a consensus decision.

If there is no consensus at this point, you need to decide how time sensitive the decision is. Often, the bigger the decision is, the better to give people time to consider it; you can always return another day to revisit the subject. However, once the point is reached when a decision must be made, the leader has the responsibility to weigh all the opinions and decide.

3.4 Decision making under certainty risk and uncertainty

People who work in project management recognize that risk is an inherent part of project delivery. If we wish to encourage risk taking, we must be prepared to accept and recognize that people will fail from time to time. Having absolute success without experiencing failure is almost impossible in project management. Yet, much can be done to mitigate risky decisions.

In the "how" of project management, there are many ways of achieving the objective. Almost by definition, none of these ways will be exclusively the right one. Each will have its own distinct strengths and weakness, which may turn out to be opportunities or threats to the project. In practice, projects have many objectives, measures of performance and values, so that it may not always be possible to be certain of a particular outcome from all decision alternatives. A considerable amount of academic work has resulted in decision making being classified into three groups:

1. Decision making under certainty (a decision-making environment in which the future outcomes or states of nature are known).
2. Decision making under risk (a decision-making environment in which several outcomes or states of nature may occur as a result of decision or alternative. The probabilities of the outcomes or the states of nature are known).

3. Decision making under uncertainty (a decision-making environment in which several outcomes or states of nature may occur. The probabilities of these outcomes are not known).

1. Decision making under certainty

When a manager knows or is certain of all the effects of variables on an issue, "certainty" exists. This means that the manager should be able to make accurate decisions when these circumstances exist. Of course, this type of decision-making environment is rare.

The issues associated with this technique are that it assumes all outcomes are known with certainty. It also presupposes that the decision maker will act and behave in a rational manner, which may not be the case in practice.

2. Decision making under risk

Decision making under risk assumes implicitly that for each possible alternative, the probability of occurrence is known. The decision process allows the decision maker to evaluate alternative tactics prior to making any decision. The process is as follows:

- The problem is defined and all feasible alternatives are considered. The possible outcomes for each alternative are evaluated.
- Outcomes are discussed based on their expected monetary payoffs (EMP) or net gain in reference to assets or time.
- Various uncertainties are quantified in terms of probabilities.
- The quality of the optimal strategy depends upon the quality of the judgements. The decision maker should identify and examine the sensitivity of the optimal strategy with respect to the crucial factors.

Whenever the decision maker has some knowledge regarding the states of nature, they may be able to assign subjective probability estimates for the occurrence of each state. In such cases, the problem is classified as decision making under risk. The situation requires estimating the probability that one or more known variables might influence the decision made. If the basis for the decision is stated in terms of maximizing results, for example, service levels, the decision maker would select the alternative that produces the best result. However, if the basis for the decision is stated in terms of minimizing the outcome, for example, costs, the decision maker would select the alternative that minimizes the results.

3. Decision making under uncertainty

A condition of uncertainty exists when a project manager is faced with reaching a decision with no historical data concerning the variables and/or unknowns and their probability of occurrence. In these circumstances, the manager can decide:

- To maximize the possible results
- To minimize the results
- To maximize the results that are the minimum possible under the circumstances
- To minimize the maximum possible results
- To avoid or delay the decision.

Two of the better-known approaches that can be used for decision making under uncertainty are: (1) Maximin and maximax and (2) Savage's regret criterion.

Maximin and maximax: decision rule suggests, the maximum decision criteria indicate that the decision maker should select the alternative, which maximizes the maximum value of the outcome. The maximax criterion is often referred to as *optimistic approach* as it implies that the decision maker expects the best to occur. For example, when individuals choose between lottery tickets (or scratch cards), the lottery that offers the highest possible prize appears to be particularly attractive, even though this lottery offers very few medium-size prizes. This is in line with a maximax type of decision behaviour. By contrast, there is extensive empirical evidence concerning the willingness to purchase insurance, which suggests a maximin type of decision behaviour.

Savage's regret criterion is defined as: "The regret of an outcome is equal to the difference between the value of that outcome and the maximum value of the outcome possible, for the particular chance events that occur (Harrison, 1983). In simple terms individuals know that when they make a decision they will regret if they make the wrong decision. They thus take this anticipated regret into account when they decide. This is probably what makes them loss averse. When thinking ahead, managers may experience anticipatory regret, as they realize that they may regret in the future. This can be a powerful dissuader or can create a specific motivation to do one thing in order to avoid something else.

The following summary illustrates the main points discussed in Section 3.4.

- Decision making is traditionally classified into three areas: certainty, risk, and uncertainty.
- Each classification has an array of techniques, which can be used to analyse a decision problem.
- Decision makers have a fundamental aversion to risk.
- The important values to be considered need not necessarily be the criterion of EMP but may be the utility of outcomes.

3.5 Decision audits and reviews

As previously stated not all decisions made by managers turn out to be good decisions. Indeed many of "us" need to make a few bad decisions to gain experience and improve our judgement. It is, however, important both for the individual and the organization that we learn from mistakes (or errors of judgement). Because we are human, our personalities influence how we react to feedback, and although the project team may be the best source of information about how the project was undertaken or how we performed as project managers – it may not be impartial or diplomatic in its feedback. For these reasons organizations should make arrangements to undertake periodic assessments of the project.

Decision audits or reviews should be carried out to independently assess the decision-making performance of decision makers in order to improve accountability and facilitate future decision making by those with the responsibility to oversee or initiate projects. Audits or reviews can help to provide credibility to the management systems and reporting of project managers as they objectively verify and evaluate decision performance.

The type of audit or review to be conducted depends on the objectives of the audit. It can be an audit to assess the decision-making performance of the project manager or it can be an audit to look at the project budget to see how the funds were utilized and what decisions were made in utilizing those funds. It can be a combination of the two, or it can have a specific purpose such as looking at internal control mechanisms.

Carrying out a decision audit is not just about fulfilling an internal requirement to the project, its stakeholders, and the management. Being aware of the extent of poor decision making should be a continuous process and any audit strategy should recognize this fact. Undertaking a decision audit and producing "lessons learned reports" gives the organization an opportunity to:

- Engage with project stakeholders
- Review activity and performance
- Plan for future change in decision making
- Make sure that the lessons learned are put into the broader context of the project plans and strategies

Increasing engagement in decision audit initiatives:

- Provides valuable information and knowledge
- Reflects the objective of helping individuals to take control and responsibility of their decisions.

Individuals rarely experience single-issue problems – problems are generally "cross-cutting" in scope and solution. Given this situation organizations should:

- Identify joint approaches and strategies for tackling decisions
- Make sure that resources are identified and used appropriately
- Understand the relationship between problems in order to target their activities to tackle issues.

Unless legal restrictions or ethical considerations prevent it, audit reports should be made public to all individuals within the organization. This helps to increase transparency of management and its oversight. It also increases accountability through the wide dissemination of information so that the project stakeholders and project managers can assess the integrity of the findings.

3.6 Chapter summary – 10 key points

The most important points to take away from this chapter are:

1. Making decisions is by and large what project managers do. How well (or effectively) they make such decisions will be based on the criteria of behavioural history, situational beliefs, personal values, social and occupational norms, personality, and environmental constraints.
2. The basis for choosing a particular way for implementing a decision is not governed merely by considerations of conventional logic or rationality. Decisions are also likely to involve considerations of justice and fairness as perceived by various stakeholders and by considerations of personal ethics or morality as perceived by different persons.

3. The most important resource whose limitations have to be considered is people who carry out the decision. No decision can be better than the people who have to carry it out. Their vision, competence, skill, and understanding determine what they can and cannot do.

4. Depending on the tools and techniques used, decision making can either be time wasting or it can be the project manager's best means of finding the right question and the answers to it.

5. Despite some limitations, brainstorming remains a popular technique. For many groups, it has provided a first clear picture of their potential to think creatively together and to move off in new directions. Since brainstorming is an expansive, divergent thinking approach that generates lots of ideas, it needs to be followed by a narrowing, focussing activity that extracts a reasonable number of promising ideas for the group to work with.

6. The way in which decisions are made in any project or group depends on the power structure and nature of the group leadership. The way in which a decision has been reached can have a profound effect on our confidence and trust.

7. Some decision-making strategies involve only the project manager or a few persons in a somewhat unilateral mode while others involve the entire team through discussion.

8. The search for consensus agreement relies on every person in the team bringing their best self forward to seek unity. The group need not all think the same, have the same opinion, or support the same proposal in a unanimous vote.

9. If we wish to encourage risk taking, we must be prepared to accept and recognize that people will fail from time to time. Having absolute success without experiencing failure is almost impossible in project management.

10. Decision audits or reviews should be carried out to independently assess the decision-making performance of decision makers in order to improve accountability and facilitate future decision making by those with the responsibility to oversee or initiate projects.

3.7 Next chapter

In the next chapter we will explore some of the leadership issues associated with power and conflict. We will examine influencing strategies and how such strategies may be used to counter political threats. We will also explore sources of power and interpersonal conflict and review some conflict resolution strategies.

Chapter references and further reading

Adair, J. (1989) Great Leaders, Guildford, Talbart and Adair Press.

Beach, L.R. (1990) Image Theory: Decision Making in Personal and Organizational Context, England, John Wiley & Sons.

Drucker, P. (1954) The Practice of Management, New York, Harper & Row.

George, A. (1980) Presidential Decision Making in Foreign Policy: The Effective Use of Information and Advice, Westview, USA.

Harrison, P. (1983) Operational Research, Core Business Studies, London, Mitchell Beazley Publishers.

Harrison, F.E. (1987) The Managerial Decision-Making Process, Boston, MA, Houghton Mifflin Company.

Jensen, J.V. (1978) A heuristic for the analysis of the nature and extent of a problem, The Journal of Creative Behavior 12(2): 168–180.

Kepner, C.H. and B.B. Tregoe (1981) The New Rational Manager, Princeton, NJ, Princeton Research Press.

McManus, J. and T. Wood-Harper (2003) Information Systems Project Management: Methods, Tools and Techniques, Upper Saddle River, NJ, Pearson Education (Prentice Hall).

*Simon, H. (1977) The New Science of Management Decision, Englewood Cliffs, NJ, Prentice Hall.

4 Leadership Influence, Power, and Conflict Management

4.1 Influencing the leadership challenge

In Chapter 1 (Section 1.5.1), it was stated that project managers thrive on achieving something important and being in a position of influencing others to achieve. In a complex project environment, leadership involves more than taking control and making decisions. Effective leaders recognize the importance of building support for decisions by engaging the stakeholders and affected interests in the management process. As discussed in Chapter 2, engagement allows the project manager to involve key stakeholders, interest groups, and a myriad of intertwined interests. Without engagement, there is a risk that today's solutions will become tomorrow's problems. Involving affected parties in problem solving and decision-making efforts can minimize this risk. In many instances, consensus-based processes are the most effective approach to resolving conflicts.

Influencing others begins with this engagement process. To deliver successful projects, project managers need to work "smart". In shaping strategy and policy decisions, working smart means ensuring that there is broad-based support for the project, so that you do not spend limited resources defending unsupported initiatives or forcing unwanted programmes on resistant individuals. This can be avoided by working collaboratively with and influencing stakeholders when addressing contentious strategic or policy issues. Collaborative processes secure the support of stakeholders and help ensure the development of creative and durable policies and work programmes. As Feld notes:

In the next few years, the importance of influence and persuasion skills for CIO's will only grow. Leading other executives to a full understanding of the game-changing nature of IT will require a planned approach to influencing. Involve other execs in IT decisions to get their buy-in, and customize your approach for each person. There are limits to your personal influence; only by persuading others to support your course can you move the organization in the right direction in its use of technology.
(Source: Charlie Feld, IT Leadership 2010: The skills that CIO's will need to win the game, CIO, 2003)

Research suggests that the use of influencing strategies within management has been used successfully on a diverse range of issues (Manning and Robertson, 2003). Organizations are increasingly turning to collaborative approaches to address today's complex and often contentious business issues. Collaborative and influencing approaches allow parties with a stake in an issue to create solutions that are agreeable to all. The act of creating mutually satisfying solutions establishes a sense of ownership. Because of this, the stakeholders are more likely to support and implement the solutions (McManus, 2005).

Many writers have stated that fundamental to an understanding of behaviour in team work is an understanding of the nature of influence. What then is influence? Influence can be described as "the key feature of leadership, performed through communicating, decision making, and motivation". At the heart of influencing is "relationship" and influencing others to some degree is born out of the interdependent relationships we have with other people. It is because people are interdependent that they must communicate and develop constructive relationships with peers and stakeholders. Strong relationships make influencing easier but they can impose constraints in that they can create power differentials.

Part of the problem with stakeholder management is that it is often primarily shaped by the knowledge of those who operate at macro levels. Without an adequate understanding of the local situation, we will not know whether our influencing measures are likely to be appropriate, and the perspectives and interests of local stakeholders often end up being cut out. This clearly has implications for creating strategies and policies that move the project forward. Any influencing strategy is likely to have several different objectives at the same time, for instance, tackling budgets, managing resources, or increasing economic opportunities. Where aims are multiple, there will inevitably be some measure of trade-off between objectives. It will not be possible to pursue and maximize one exclusively. This can be a problem for those project managers who are used to concentrating on a single variable: this generally demands a new approach and way of thinking.

A strategic approach to influencing others is one that recognizes that the world changes fast, and that there is much about the project environment in which one is operating that is not known. Given this, influencing strategies cannot be a simple matter of designing and implementing definitive blueprints. Project managers need to admit that they are dealing with provisional knowledge, and aims and methods need to be tested and revaluated along the way. What looked like the right strategic goal and method a month ago may not seem that way further down the line. New voices and understandings may emerge that require rethinking and redesigning of a strategy or policy.

4.2 Methods of influence and persuasion

The influencer's basic fear is the loss of social approval and those skilled at influencing recognize that different topics and situations have to be handled differently. Use the wrong style, about the wrong subject, at the wrong time and you will create resistance or get a response entirely different to the one you wanted. What project managers should be looking for when influencing others is win/win outcomes. After influencing, there are four general methods to win others to your way of thinking: persuasion, mental conditioning, manipulation, and brainwashing. All are equally powerful, but the last two are negative and can have serious repercussions. It is important to our success that we learn how to effectively influence and persuade, but it is equally important to our well-being that we learn how to recognize manipulation and brainwashing. Mental conditioning is considered neutral and can be positive or negative depending on how it is used.

4.2.1 Persuasion

To persuade another is to induce to undertake a course of action or embrace a point of view by means of argument, reasoning, or entreaty. Persuasion is more assertive than influence, but may prove more effective at times. Despite persuasion's definition, argumentation should be avoided when persuading. Clear reasoning is the most effective form of persuasion for getting your points across. Open-minded individuals will often say "convince me", in which they are basically asking to be presented with facts and reasoning so that they too can share your belief.

The ancient Greeks had a grounded approach to persuasion. A Greek citizen could hire a Sophist to help him learn to argue. (Sophists were itinerant lecturers and writers devoted to knowledge – you might say they were the graduate students of the ancient world.) The sophists argued that persuasion was a useful tool to discover the truth. They believed that the process of arguing and debating would expose bad ideas and allow the good ones to be revealed. Sophists did not particularly care which side of an issue he was arguing. The stated goal was reasoned argument that exposed the truth. They believed in the free market of good ideas and the power of words.

In persuasion, the way we use words is critical. We can encourage or discourage people, open them up or close them to us; we can motivate and inspire or dampen enthusiasm and engender doubts. We need to engage people and ask questions that will involve people in the communication process (Chapter 5). In persuading people to our point of view, we must ask the right questions that stimulate thinking. Research would suggest that many people do not know how to ask good questions. Many people prefer to talk than to listen, and the fact is good listeners are exceedingly rare. Furthermore, when people think about persuasion, in general, it takes the form of advice "What I think you should do is . . ." Advice may be appropriate in some situations, but it undoubtedly is far overused. Unfortunately, because of its low ownership nature, it is also probably undervalued.

4.2.2 Mental conditioning

Mental conditioning is a technique one often uses on oneself to change a belief or create a feeling using repetition. Some common examples of this are prayer, mantras, and affirmations. Mental conditioning can also be used on others. The best-known example of this is advertising. Advertisers use mental conditioning to associate a positive feeling with their product. Through repeated exposure, our minds are conditioned to accept the association.

Eischens states "conditioning is learning based on the consequences produced by the responses of elicited behavior". Simply put, environment affects our behaviour. If what we do produces a desired consequence, we do it again. If what we do produces undesired consequences, we try not to do it again. We learn by operating on the environment. Eischens used the example of words to illustrate this point. As she states, "words that elicit positive emotional responses reinforce the speaker to utter them again in order to receive the positive response". This is interesting because there have been several studies on the use of nuisance words, the emotional release caused by their utterances and the subsequent overuse of them (Carlson and Buskist, 1997).

4.2.3 Manipulation

To manipulate another is to use shrewd or devious management, especially for one's own advantage. Simply put, the main difference between influencing another and manipulating them is intent. Those who use manipulation do so only thinking about what they want, not about the wants of those they manipulate. It is not easy to detect when you are being manipulated. Take the following example.

A manager was conducting an appraisal interview with his subordinate who said "I like working here but I don't find the job stretches me very much as I have now got things well organized". The manager replied "But I think productivity in your area could be improved". The subordinate immediately went on the defensive, explaining why productivity has been restricted owing to illness and absenteeism. The appraisal ended and the subordinate said to a colleague afterwards "It was a waste of time. He just talked about what he wanted to pick on and did not listen to what I was concerned about. I told him the job bored me and didn't stretch me any more but he just ignored what I wanted to talk about".

Once again, we must rely on our common sense to help us distinguish between influence and manipulation. By recognizing the signs and signals, you are helping to reduce the risk of manipulation. Some of the clearest indicators come from people's nonverbal behaviour (or body language), for example, the pointed finger to emphasize a point, the hands over the mouth to guard against the wrong word, or the eyes looking upward for help. Nonverbal signs and signals take different forms.

4.2.4 Brainwashing

The term *brainwashing* was first used by the news correspondent Hunter in 1951 to describe the conversion process that American

POWs had undergone in Chinese prison camps during the Korean War. He translated the term from the Chinese concept of *hse nao*, "wash brain". Actually, Mao Tse-tung used the term *ssu-hsiang tou-cheng*, or "thought struggle", as early as 1929 to denote what we now commonly refer to as "mind control", "thought reform", or "thought control" (Singer, 1995).

The dictionary defines brainwashing as a "process of systematically, forcibly, and intensively, indoctrinating a person to destroy or weaken his or her beliefs and ideas so that he becomes willing to accept different or opposite beliefs or ideas". I do not fully agree with this definition because one cannot be "forced" to accept a belief; this contradicts the entire concept of free will. One can, however, be forced to live by another's belief, against his or her own will. Remove the word "forcibly" and that is brainwashing in a nutshell. The key element to brainwashing is the creation of an environment where questioning, doubt, reason, creativity, thinking for oneself, and dissent are discouraged or even punished.

According to Bo Bennett, the ability to win others to your way of thinking is a key element of both leadership and success. There are just as many ways to do it wrong as there are to do it right. As a successful leader, use positive influence often and gentle persuasion when necessary. Use mental conditioning on yourself to abolish limiting beliefs or to instil empowering beliefs. Never use manipulation or brainwashing in an attempt to win others to your way of thinking and be aware when others attempt to use these techniques on you.

(Section 4.2 is in part based on the teachings of Bo Bennett and some text is reproduced with permission from the paper "Winning others to your way of thinking".)

4.3 Influencing strategies, tactics, and styles

With respect to resources and finance, most project managers find themselves in a quandary at one time or another on how to acquire such resources. The best way to address this conundrum is through a thoughtful and tactical use of influence. To use influence in a tactical manner requires forethought. A typical approach is to first clearly identify what you need accomplished. Then, seek out the managers that you need to influence.

To some degree, the type of influencing strategy (or tactics) to be adopted will be governed by the specific situation and culture of the organization in which the individual project manager is operating. Equally, different styles may be adopted according to the demands of that situation.

In any large organization, there will be many individuals hoping to influence events. Such individuals thrive on challenge and can exist at the highest levels of power by getting you to think things and to do things they want you to think and do. Most people are either unaware of these influences or vastly overestimate the amount of freedom they have to make up their own minds. But successful influencers know that if they can manage the situation and choose the correct strategy, your response to their technique will be as reliable as Christmas Day.

Marwell and Schmitt (1967) developed a taxonomy of 16 influence tactics (Table 4.1). It is a "classic" taxonomy that inspired a lot of subsequent research, writing, and thinking about the topic of influence. In essence, these 16 influencing tactics can actually be grouped together in five factors representing the strategies that might be used: rewarding activity, punishing activity, expertise, activation of personal commitments, and activation of impersonal commitments. The suggestion here is that, in the agreement setting, a person facing pressure is likely to make a choice for behaviour on the basis of one or more of these five strategies.

When you create a "win/win" situation, you will start to win. But, no matter how talented an influencer you may be, "experience"

Table 4.1 Marwell and Schmitt taxonomy of influence tactics

Tactic	Example after Genece Hamby
1. Reward: if the receiver complies there will be a reward	I will reward you if you do it. "I will throw in a pair of speakers if you buy it today." "Thanks! I will make certain your manager knows how helpful you were."
2. Punishment: issues an ultimatum for, compliance, saying do this or be punished	I will punish you if you do not do it. "If you do not buy it today, I will not be able to offer you this special incentive price again." "If I cannot get it at that price tomorrow, then I will take my business elsewhere."
3. Positive expertise: compliance will assure a reward due to the nature of the situation	Speaking as an authority on the subject. "I can tell you that rewards will occur if you do X, because of the nature of reality." "If you start working out at our gym regularly, you will find that people are more attracted to you physically."

Table 4.1 (Continued)

Tactic	Example after Genece Hamby
4. Negative expertise: states the opposite of expertise (positive); with an outcome of punishment for not complying	Speaking as an authority on the subject. "I can tell you that punishments will occur if you do Y, because of the nature of reality." "If you do not buy it today, you may never get another chance – our stock is almost sold out."
5. Liking, ingratiation: suggests that the sender acts friendly and helpful to put the receiver in a positive, likewise, helpful mood of compliance	Getting the prospect into a good frame of mind. "Gosh! you look nice today. I just love that hat you are wearing!" "Should we order dessert before we look over the contracts?"
6. Gifting, pregiving: offers a reward before the compliance is requested	Giving something as a gift, before requesting compliance. The idea is that the target will feel the need to reciprocate later. "Here is a little something we thought you would like. Now about those contracts . . ."
7. Debt: places guilt on the receivers, requiring compliance for past favours the sender has performed	Calling in past favours. "After all I have done for you! Come on – *this* time it is *me* who needs the favour."
8. Aversive stimulation: condones punishment until the receiver agrees to comply	Continuous punishment and the cessation of punishment are contingent on compliance. "I am going to play my classical music at full volume if you insist on playing your rock music at full volume. When you turn yours down, I will turn mine down."
9. Moral appeal: suggests the receiver is immoral for noncompliance	This tactic entails finding moral common ground, and then using the moral commitments of a person to obtain compliance. "You believe that women should get equal pay for equal work, do you not? You do not believe that men are better than women, do you? Then you ought to sign this petition! It is the right thing to do."
10. Positive self-feeling: promotes a boost in self-esteem if the receiver complies	You will feel better if you X. "If you join our club today, you will feel better about yourself because you will know that you are improving every day."

Table 4.1 (Continued)

Tactic	Example after Genece Hamby
11. Negative self-feeling: reverses the situation, making the receiver feel worse about themselves for not complying	You will feel bad if you Y. "If you do not return it to him and apologize, you will find it hard to live with yourself."
12. Positive altercasting: hints that a "good" person would comply	Good people do X. "Smart people tend to sign up for the year in advance, because that is how they can get the best weekly rate."
13. Negative altercasting: makes the receiver that only a "bad" person would fail to comply	Only a bad person would do Y. "You are not like those bad sports who whine and complain when they lose a game."
14. Altruism: asks the receiver to comply due to the sender's desperate situation	Do-Me-A-Favour. "I really need this photocopied right away, can you help me out?" (An extremely common influence tactic and in wide use among friends and acquaintances.)
15. Positive esteem of others: says the receiver will be valued as a better person for complying	Other people will think more highly of you if you X. "People respect a man who drives a Mercedes."
16. Negative esteem of others: says that people will look down upon the receiver if they choose not to comply	Other people will think worse of you if you Y. "You do not want people thinking that you are a drug-head loser, do you?"

would suggest that you may not always get a win/win outcome or persuade people to your point of view. By opening their minds, however, to constructive attitudes and effective courses of action, you may eventually win them over.

4.4 The cultural power game in leadership

An understanding of culture, and how to act within it, is a crucial skill for project managers trying to achieve strategic outcomes for their projects. From our discussion in Chapter 1, leaders have the best perspective, because of their position in the organization, to see the dynamics of the culture, what is, what should remain, and what needs transformation. This is the essence of strategic and project success. A distinguished MIT Professor of Management, Edgar Schein, author of *Organizational Culture and Leadership: A Dynamic View* (1988), suggests that an organization's culture develops to help it cope with its environment. Today, organizational leaders are confronted with many complex issues during their attempts to generate organizational achievement in project environments. A project manager's success will depend, to a great extent, upon understanding organizational culture and the power bases within the organization.

Schein contends that many of the problems confronting leaders can be traced to their inability to analyse and evaluate organizational cultures. Many leaders, when trying to implement new strategies or a strategic plan leading to a new vision, will discover that their strategies will fail if they are inconsistent with the organization's culture. A leader who comes into an organization prepared to "shake the organization up" and institute sweeping changes, often experiences resistance to changes and failure. Difficulties with organizational transformations arise from failures to analyse an organization's existing culture.

Schein offers the potential leader the following advice:

1. Don't oversimplify culture or confuse it with climate, values, or corporate philosophy. Culture *underlies* and largely *determines* these other variables. Trying to change values or climate without getting at the underlying culture will be a futile effort.
2. Don't label culture as solely a human resources (read "touchy–feely") aspect of an organization, affecting only its human side. The impact of culture goes far beyond the human side of the organization to affect and influence its basic mission and goals.
3. Don't assume that the leader can manipulate culture as he or she can control many other aspects of the organization. Culture, because it is largely determined and controlled by the members of the organization, not the leaders, is different. Culture may end up controlling the leader rather than being controlled by him or her.
4. Don't assume that there is a "correct" culture, or that a strong culture is better than a weak one. It should be apparent that different cultures may fit different organizations

and their environments, and that the desirability of a strong culture depends on how well it supports the organization's strategic goals and objectives.

5. Don't assume that all the aspects of an organization's culture are important, or that it will have a major impact on the functioning of the organization. Some elements of an organization's culture may have little impact on its functioning, and the leader must distinguish which elements are important, and focus on those.

Numerous studies of organizational culture (and uses of power) have highlighted that the formation and maintenance of culture requires interpersonal interaction within subgroups. For example, research led by Louis (1983) demonstrated the benefits of subgroup interaction to newcomers "learning the ropes" of the job. Survey respondents in their first job experience reported that the three most important socialization aids were:

- Interaction with peers
- Interaction with their managers
- Interaction with senior co-managers.

Interaction with peers on the job is viewed as most important in helping new project managers become effective employees. Interaction is important for the acculturation of new project managers. However, to get a grasp on how power bases are formed and promulgated, we need to ask, "What is the content of interpersonal interaction and sources of power in the work environment?"

4.5 Sources of power

One of the lessons learnt from reading political, management, and business biographies is that those who maintain power and influence over protracted periods of time do so because they are conscious of how power is developed and what its sources are, and because they work to acquire and maintain these sources through planned effort.

Since managers are largely concerned with influencing others, it seems appropriate that they should be characterized by the need for power. Managers who strive hard for power can be counted on to reach positions of authority over others. Individual managers who lack this drive are not likely to act in ways that will enable them to advance far up the managerial hierarchy. In the competitive struggle to attain and hold high office in management, a project manager's desire for status must be reinforced by the satisfaction and experience one gets from exercising the power and authority of high office.

Rosabeth Moss-Kanter (1985), writing in *The Change Masters*, describes power as "the ability to get things done". Although such a definition is straightforward, it has significant appeal in relation to the role of project managers. It is particularly helpful since much of the skill of a project manager revolves around the ability to manage the political power dimensions within and around the stakeholder community, so much so that failure to understand and control the political process has been the downfall of many good project managers. Politics is concerned with the way in which managers gain and use power and involve them in a range of activities, such as bargaining for resources, striking deals, forming coalitions with others, and so on. Clearly it is important for a project manager to have political skills in order to gain and keep power. Based on his own personal experience and analysis, Nicocolo Machiavelli (Gauss, 1980) advised political leaders on how to acquire power, resist dissent, and control subordinates. Machiavelli's cynical view of his fellow man is best summed up by his comment: "Men are in general ungrateful, fickle, false, cowardly, covetous, but as long as you succeed, they are yours entirely." For this reason, Machiavelli warns that when power is at stake, questions of morality are irrelevant – lying, deceit, and manipulation are all legitimate tactics.

From Machiavelli's perspective, winning the game by whatever means (power or otherwise) is all that matters. Power, however, is relative in the sense that the source of the project managers' power lie not in themselves, but in their followers. Project managers can only exercise the power that their followers allow.

Social and behavioural researchers have identified several frameworks of power. The four major types of power that individuals develop or acquire are personal, legitimate, expert, and political power. Each of these forms of power is explained here.

1. *Personal power.* Personal power (or referent power) is possessed by certain individuals and is sometimes termed *charismatic power*. Some project managers have immense charisma and are able to build powerful personal relationships with senior managers and others. Other stakeholder groups look to these types of people to make decisions for them – they can be very forceful and determined. Project

managers who use this type of power tend to sense the needs of their followers and provide a focus that meets those needs.

2. *Legitimate power.* This is based on people having positions within a structured framework. In a particular culture, power will be delegated to different managers. Since the manager's power is seen as being legitimately held, it will be accepted by others. The rights of the manager's role include the right to information, which may come from above or below that organization level, the right of access to organizational decision-making bodies (for example, project boards and steering committees), and the right to organize work activities.

3. *Expert power.* Most information technology professionals are labelled *knowledge workers*. Expert power is based on the specialist knowledge possessed by certain individuals. It frequently arises when there is complex knowledge that can be gained only through professional training and education. In essence, expert power stems from, say, project managers having knowledge and skill in an area (for example, object development) that other managers do not. Other managers will be willing to accept the project manager's influence in the field of the project manager's expertise. Expert power in areas that are crucial to the attainment of success may give the power holder an important role with its associated position source. So, if the project manager's expertise is questioned by one of the stakeholders, it may be possible for him to resort to the methods associated with legitimate power. The level of expert power exercised will be related to the degree to which the individual can be substituted. If the person is difficult to replace, he or she is likely to be in a very strong position.

4. *Political power.* Political power stems from being supported by a stakeholder group. To gain political power, the project manager will need to be able to work with people and social systems so that he can gain support and allegiance from them. Gaining true political power involves having an understanding of those factors most likely to encourage others to support you, as well as understanding how systems can be used in your favour. Political leadership also involves having access to sanctions and rewards. A number of tactics can be employed to obtain and retain political power. For example, project managers can develop formal and informal contacts with a stakeholder group, which will enhance their personal power base.

5. *Goodwill power.* Goodwill power is generated by individuals using their positive relationship with others to impose change. Goodwill power exists in relationships wherein two or more persons have been able to establish trust with one another.

6. *Reward power.* Reward power is generated as one provides access to resources necessary to perform a job. Those using reward power may take actions that ensure that others believe that they will use resources to reward them. Persons who employ resource power to influence others must have some control over spending, hiring, space, and informational decisions. Other types of rewards include providing visibility, access, or priorities.

(Points 1–4 are taken from McManus and Wood-Harper (2003), Information Systems Project Management, p. 53.)

4.6 Managing with power

In Chapter 2 of the book *Managing with Power,* Jeffrey Pfeffer suggests that "power" is used more frequently under conditions of moderate interdependence. According to Pfeffer, it is important to develop power and influence when people with whom you are interdependent have a different point of view than you, and thus cannot be relied upon to do what you want. Interdependence results from many things, including the way in which tasks are organized. One factor that is critical in affecting the nature and the amount of interdependence is the scarcity of resources. Slack resources reduce interdependence, while scarcity increases it. As an example, consider the case of job promotions. If an organization is growing rapidly and there are promotional opportunities, the competition for promotions will be less intense.

Project managers have to operate and survive in many worlds and are reliant to some degree on the "good will" of other peer managers. Some academics have argued that a comprehensive view of the interdependence of a manager–manager relationship should include not only interdependence (relative power) but also total interdependence (or total power). The total interdependence refers to the intensity of a relationship. A high level of total interdependence is an indicator of a strong, cooperative long-term relationship in which both managers have invested. Like "good will power", mutual trust and mutual commitment characterize these relationships. Besides loyalty towards the other party and the accompanying desire to continue the relationship, there is an alternative motivation for both parties to keep the partnership intact. In the case that both parties know that the other party possesses much power, it is not likely that either side is going to use it. The risk of retaliation is often considered to be too high. In addition, when total interdependence is high, both managers are faced with high exit barriers. In accordance with the teachings of Bacharach and Lawler (1981), we may measure total interdependence in a relationship by "the sum" of the managers' dependence on one another.

As discussed in Chapter 2, although power is inherent in a given formal position, leaders cannot maintain authority unless followers are prepared to believe in that authority. In a sense, leadership is conferred by followers. As previously pointed out, it is not enough to know the sources of power or that power exists. It is also critical to know how power may be used and to have an armoury of strategies and tactics that translate power and influence into practical results. One such strategy is power sharing.

4.6.1 Power sharing

Power sharing is a strategy to resolve difference of opinions over who should have the power. Instead of fighting over who should have power over whom, power sharing relies upon the joint exercise of power. If conflicts can be reframed to focus on how such power sharing might take place, they can become much more constructive.

Power sharing can take a variety of forms. One approach is to grant minority groups autonomy over some – or all – aspects of their own affairs. This autonomy can be limited to cultural issues: religion and education for example, or it can be extended to cover the social, economic, and political spheres as well. At the extreme, it can take the form of granting complete independence and allowing a minority group to form its own sovereign nation state.

Another approach to power sharing is more integrative. Governance is handled by leaders from each group who work jointly and cooperatively to make decisions and resolve conflicts. This approach relies on ethically neutral decision making and policies.

Implementing either approach is usually difficult, as groups holding power are reluctant to relinquish that power, and groups without it tend to want massive change to occur more quickly than the dominant group is likely to accept. For this reason, demands for power sharing and autonomy often ferment conflict more than they resolve it. However, if minority groups can frame their demands in a way that emphasizes joint benefit, and focus on developing a mutually acceptable way of achieving self-determination for all groups, they are likely to meet with more success than if they were to take a more combative or competitive approach.

4.6.2 Maintaining power

Niccolo Machiavelli wrote his famous dissertation on power, *The Prince*, in 1517. According to him the purpose of power is to maintain itself and to extend itself. It has nothing to do with the welfare of the people. It has nothing to do with principles or ideology, or right and wrong. The welfare of people, principles, ideology, right and wrong: these are related to the means to the end, but the goal is power. Do whatever it takes to keep your power and extend your power.

Machiavelli notes "Men will succeed as long as method and fortune are in harmony." If not they stand to lose all they have gained. Machiavelli promoted the idea that a ruler (leader) should be gentle most of the time, but when necessary the ruler must make use of any form of manipulation, deceit, and even murder to achieve his ends.

People in power are seldom challenged or given bad news, and even when challenged, they have a tendency to reject the discrepant information. It is no wonder, then, that changing circumstances often produce, with some lag, a dynamic that causes those in power to lose that power (Pfeffer, 1992). To avoid losing power, project managers (or leaders) should be sensitive to subtle changes in the political, economic, and social environment, and understand how a particular management style, or a particular set of actions jeopardize their position and power base.

(Quotations are taken from Machiavelli (1990) The Prince, ed. Quentin Skinner and Russell Price [Cambridge: Cambridge University Press].)

4.7 Managing conflict

Conflict may be described as a struggle resulting from incompatible or opposing desires. It could be argued that a manager's view of the cause of conflict is encouraged by the perspective offered by the classical theory, which is largely related to the breakdown of formal authority linked to legitimate power and the need for measures to maintain such power and restore it when need be.

In some respects, management sees the occurrence of conflict as a rejection of its legitimate right to govern and control. As a consequence, conflict is identified as abnormal behaviour and, therefore, is likely to result in punishment for the perpetrators of deviant behaviour. In some respects, this supports the view that management is based on a "unitary view", which carries with it the expectations that everyone within the organization shares the same view, works together as a team, acknowledges the legitimacy of hierarchy, and respects senior management. Anything that appears to interfere with this view is considered "bad" for business and is dealt with according to the rules, procedures, customs, and conventions that exist within a particular organization.

4.7.1 Causes of conflict

As stated earlier, conflict results from incompatible or opposing desires. Conflict is a natural outcome of human interaction. Conflict exists whenever there is a disagreement and derives from differences in attitudes, beliefs, and expectations. As described earlier, conflict can result from not acknowledging management authority or legitimacy or lack of differences in perception as to what has happened or what needs to be done. Whenever two or more people disagree about a decision or action, conflict exists. Conflict is inevitable because not all persons think alike, hold the same values or priorities, or react alike to situations.

The project manager should recognize the difference between resolving conflict and managing conflict. The goal of conflict resolution is conflict elimination. Conflict resolution is often an impossible task and not always a desirable goal. Project managers who accept conflict resolution as their ultimate objective will undoubtedly fail. Conflict management is directed towards reducing destructive conflict but allows for the existence of constructive conflict. Project managers who accept conflict management as the objective realize that all conflict cannot or should not be eliminated.

Although there are many causes of conflict, I would like to discuss two. These are the conflict between managers and managed, and the conflict between individuals.

4.7.1.1 Conflict between manager and managed

Conflict between the project manager and those that are managed is more likely to occur when communication is not clear and when there is confusion about what is valued and rewarded. It is the responsibility of the project manager to make goals and expectations clear. It is imperative that the project manager translates the more general project and client expectations into activities and achievements that are discipline specific.

In my experience, conflict between those who manage and are managed tends to be an issue in the early phases of a project and issues tend to centre on time, cost, and resource priorities. These three attributes create tension between parties because project managers have limited control over external risks that are likely to impact these areas. Keeping the project objective clearly in mind goes a long way towards minimizing disruptive conflicts as does involving personnel directly affected by the decisions made by the project manager. Table 4.2 outlines some sources of project conflict.

4.7.1.2 Conflict between individuals

Conflict between individuals occurs when they operate under different value systems. Some individuals prefer to see themselves as responding purely to the demands of their own set of values. The view of another's value system and position is probably the greatest block to handling conflict between individuals constructively. Some of the more common misrepresentations can be found in almost all conflicting positions between individuals, groups, and organizations. Three of these misrepresentations are:

Mirror image: All individuals think that they are innocent victims representing truth and justice. Each may see the other person as "the enemy". Each perceives himself or herself as totally right; the other as totally wrong. The position of such individuals is "Everything I do is right; everything you do is wrong."

Tunnel vision: Individuals can see clearly the underhanded, slanted, or false and vicious acts of others while being totally blind to the same behaviour in them. This position is described as "What is okay for me to do is not acceptable for you to do." This distortion allows a double standard, even when people are aware of the unfair actions on both sides.

Table 4.2 A–Z sources of project conflict

Source	Explanation
Communication	Conflict resulting from poor exchanges between project manager and staff. Misunderstandings of project related goals and objectives (over 90% of conflicts are attributed to faulty communication)
Costs	Conflict arises from lack of funding or who gets what part of the budget
Leadership	Conflict arises from a need for the project manager to take strategic decisions or from lack of decision making
Managerial	Conflict develops over how the project will be managed, reporting relationships and responsibilities, group relationships, project scope, and agreements
Politics	Conflict that centres on issues of power and control, or hidden agendas
Relationships	Conflict centres on interpersonal differences rather than the job in hand. This may include conflict from prejudice or stereotyping individuals
Resources	Conflict resulting from competition for resources among other project managers and projects
Technical	Conflict that arises out of technical differences of opinion

(Source: McManus and Wood-Harper, 2003).

> *Polarized thinking:* This kind of thinking happens when one or both parties have an oversimplified view of the conflict. A value judgement is involved, with one side seen as good and the other side seen as bad.

If project and other managers allow these misrepresentations to control the way they handle conflict, the issue probably will remain unresolved. The focus is on blaming the other and justifying yourself, rather than focussing on the issue at hand. The other person will almost instinctively become defensive in an attempt to justify his or her own position. The result is likely to be hostility rather than resolution. Each person in the relationship probably will see the other as overly emotional and unreasonable. The relationship ends up with more conflict rather than less.

It should also be noted that conflict, which is allowed to run its own course, is more likely to be destructive. Project managers need to be ready to manage conflict. However, two precautions must be noted. First, how a project manager responds to a conflict affects the conflict. Even when project managers opt to ignore an existing conflict, their silence affects the conflict. Second, the project manager's response is never static in that a manager brings to each conflict a personal set of beliefs, perceptions, and expectations. Project managers need to remember that their perception of the persons involved or the situation may not be congruent with reality. Everyone, including project managers, views conflict from their own bias and interests despite the best of intentions. Only by identifying the interests underlying the issues and positions, and recognizing the different levels of importance each party gives to these interests can the disputing parties create mutually satisfying, durable solutions to conflicts. Consider the following example:

Two men were quarrelling in a library. One wanted the window open; the other wanted it closed. They bickered back and forth over how much to leave it open: just a crack, halfway, threequarter. They were arguing so loudly that the librarian came over to find out what was the matter. She asked one man why he wanted the window open. He replied, "To get some fresh air." She asked the other why he wanted it closed. He said, "To avoid a draft." After thinking a moment, the librarian left, went into the next room, and threw open the window, bringing in fresh air without a draft. The two men viewed their problem as a conflict over positions and limited their discussions to those positions. If the librarian also had focussed only on the two men's stated positions of wanting the window open or closed, the dispute could not have been resolved with both men satisfying their needs. By looking instead at the men's underlying interests of fresh air and no draft, the librarian invented a mutually acceptable solution.

(Source from original material by Mary Parker-Follett and adapted by Fisher and Ury, 1981)

4.8 Conflict resolution strategies

Strategies or ways of dealing with conflict vary according to its nature. Project managers faced with the inevitability of conflict brought about by competition over resources, priorities, and objectives, and reinforced by individual or intergroup rivalry must attempt to manage this state of affairs in such away as to achieve a balance of conflict resolution.

Project managers sometimes overlook the fact that individuals in a conflict situation usually have mixed feelings. While there are hostile feelings and each wishes the other would give in, usually there is also some affection and a wish for agreement. Those misrepresentations mentioned earlier keep people from noticing the positive feelings, setting the seeds for failure. Try to avoid the defensive position and the feeling that the other person is the irrational enemy. Being defensive makes it hard to build a healthy relationship. Managers must be willing to listen to the other person's point of view and try to understand it. That does not mean you have to agree. It just means you have to try hard to understand and identify with that person's feelings. As project managers, you should avoid creating conflict over unimportant matters. If you find yourself frequently in conflict over trivial matters, you may need to seek help to find out what is underneath the hostility. It is also common sense to keep conflicts current. Old conflicts simply clutter up your relationships. Project managers do not have a monopoly on interpersonal skills, so review your interpersonal skills periodically. It is almost impossible to resolve conflict without the ability to listen well, express your feelings honestly, and avoid judging the other person. Table 4.3 suggests some guidance and strategies for managing interpersonal conflict.

4.9 Chapter summary – 10 key points

The most important points to take away from this chapter are:

1. Influencing others begins with this engagement process. To deliver successful projects, project managers need to work "smart". In shaping strategy and policy decisions, working smart means ensuring there is broad-based support for the project so that you do not spend limited resources defending unsupported initiatives or forcing unwanted programmes on resistant individuals.
2. Part of the problem with stakeholder management is that it is often primarily shaped by the knowledge of those who operate at macrolevels. Without an adequate understanding of the local situation, we will not know whether our influencing measures are likely to be appropriate, and the perspectives and interests of local stakeholders often end up being cut out.
3. A strategic approach to influencing others is one that recognizes that the world changes fast and that there is much about the project environment in which one is operating that is not known. Given this, influencing strategies cannot be a simple matter of designing and implementing definitive blueprints.

Table 4.3 Strategies for managing interpersonal conflict

Strategy 1: learn to stay calm	Whenever a hard issue comes up, do you feel overwhelmed? You just cannot think straight when you are so upset. For some people, they immediately become defensive. Learn to recognize when you first become flooded with strong emotions. Make a very conscious attempt to calm yourself down. It will not be easy. Find ways that work for you. For example, take time-outs. It can take 20 min for your body's pulse rate to become normal after conflict
Strategy 2: listen and speak nondefensively	Being defensive makes it hard to build a healthy relationship. We speak defensively when we try to defend ourselves. To speak nondefensively is to do the opposite. This strategy is not easy, especially when you feel emotionally attacked. Your instant reaction is to challenge that charge. You start with nondefensive listening. You must be willing to listen to the other person's point of view and try to understand it. That does not mean you have to agree. It just means you have to try hard to understand and identify with that person's feelings. Avoid: whining, making excuses, using phrases such as, "Yes, but", bringing past baggage and problems into the conversation. Keep the discussion focussed on the situation at hand
Strategy 3: work at supporting people	Put yourself in the other person's shoes and recognize the importance of his or her emotions. It is a real art, and it takes time. This strategy is especially important for persons who tend not to acknowledge the emotional part of a message. You may offer a very rational answer. They want to hear that you understand how they feels. You may want to start in very small ways. If there is constant tension between the two parties, it may be a big change to think about ways to support each other
Strategy 4: try and try again	It takes practice to learn any new skill: to drive, to play chess, to cook. These skills take practice to get better. Learning different communication skills takes practice also. Start small and talk nondefensively. If your counterpart does not respond positively, you still have to keep it up. Add your own sense of humour and personality to the nondefensive language. These four strategies can help defuse conflict and aid relationships. If you work hard, stay motivated, and do not let setbacks discourage you, these skills can benefit you as well as the organization and the people around you

(Source: based on the advice of Dr John Gottman and is adapted from *Why Marriages Succeed or Fail*, Simon and Schuster, 1994).

4. What project managers should be looking for when influencing others is win/win outcomes. After influencing there are four general methods to win others to your way of thinking: persuasion, mental conditioning, manipulation, and brainwashing.

5. To some degree, the type of influencing strategy (or tactics) to be adopted will be governed by the specific situation and culture of the organization in which the individual project manager is operating. Equally, different styles may be adopted according to the demands of that situation.

6. Today, organizational leaders are confronted with many complex issues during their attempts to generate organizational achievement in project environments. A project manager's success will depend, to a great extent, upon understanding organizational culture and the power bases within the organization.

7. Project managers have to operate and survive in many worlds and are reliant to some degree on the "good will" of other peer managers.

8. The project manager should recognize the difference between resolving conflict and managing conflict. The goal of conflict resolution is conflict elimination. Conflict resolution is often an impossible task and not always a desirable goal. Project managers who accept conflict resolution as their ultimate objective will undoubtedly fail. Conflict management is directed towards reducing destructive conflict but allows for the existence of constructive conflict.

9. Conflict between the project manager and those that are managed is more likely to occur when communication is not clear and when there is confusion about what is valued and rewarded. It is the responsibility of the project manager to make goals and expectations clear.

10. Project managers sometimes overlook the fact that individuals in a conflict situation usually have mixed feelings. While there are hostile feelings and each wishes the other would give in, usually there is also some affection and a wish for agreement.

4.10 Next chapter

In the next chapter, we will explore the communication and leadership interface. We will discuss the process of communication in projects and look at some of the issues related with developing effective channels of communication including some of the barriers associated with communication failure.

Chapter references

Bacharach, S. and E. Lawler (1981) Power and Politics in Organizations. San Francisco, CA, Jossey-Bass.

Carlson, N.R. and W. Buskist (1997) Psychology: The Science of Behavior (5th edition). Boston, MA, Allyn and Bacon.

Fisher, R. and W. Ury (1981) Getting to Yes: Negotiating Agreement without Giving In. Boston, MA, Houghton Mifflin Company.

Louis, M.R., B.Z. Posner, and G.N. Powell (1983) The availability of socialization practices. Personnel Psychology, 36(4), 857–866.

Manning, T. and B. Robertson (2003) Influencing and Negotiating Skills: Some Research and Reflections. Part II: Influencing Styles and Negotiating Skills. Emerald Group Publishing Limited, Vol. 35, No. 2, pp. 60–66.

Marwell, G. and D.R. Schmitt (1967) Dimension of compliance-gaining behavior: An empirical analysis. Sociometry, 30, 350–364.

McManus, J. (2005) Managing Stakeholders in Software Development Projects. Elsevier, Butterworth-Heinemann.

McManus, J. and T. Wood-Harper (2003) Information Systems Project Management: Methods, Tools and Techniques. Upper Saddle River, NJ, Pearson Education (Prentice Hall).

Moss-Kanter, R. (1985) Change Masters, New York, Simon Schuster, Inc.

Pfeffer, J. (1992) Managing with Power, Chapter 16, Boston, MA, Harvard School Press.

Schein, E.H. (1988) Organizational Culture and Leadership. San Francisco, MA, Jossey-Bass.

Singer M.T. with Janja Lalich, (1995), Cults in Our Midst, John Wiley and Sons, Inc.

The Gauss Seminars, Princeton University, 1980.

Further reading

Hamby, G. (2004) A Perception of Credibility: 16 Influencing Tactics, The Personal Branding DNA.

Morgan, R.M. and S.D. Hunt (1994) The commitment–trust theory of relationship marketing. Journal of Marketing, 58(3), 20–38.

Pfeffer, J. (1994) Managing with Power: Politics and Influence in Organizations. Boston, MA, Harvard Business School Press.

Schein, E.H. (1990) Organizational culture. American Psychologist, 45(2), 109–119.

Sterling-Livingston, J. (1971) Myth of the Well-Educated Manager, HBR, January.

5 Communication – The Leadership Interface

5.1 The communication process

People over time develop mental models of what characteristics a leader should have and how a leader should act. How a person communicates tends to leave a mental image (or impression) of what the leader is capable of accomplishing.

Result-orientated leaders (and project managers) often see themselves as catalysts or interventionists. They expect to achieve a great deal, but know they can do little without the efforts of others. Irrespective of leadership capability, all project managers need to perfect good communication skills. There is evidence to suggest that project managers who come from a technical background see communication skills in a less favourable way than those who have been appointed from client facing roles. Project managers are not generally measured or rewarded on their communication performance, which goes some way to explaining why communication is often cited as a key attribute of project failure. The most common symptoms of poor communication amongst the project management community are confusion or misunderstanding, duplication of effort or demand, and delay. Further consequences of poor communication include demotivation, inefficiency, and lost opportunity (see for example Turner, 1993; McManus and Wood-Harper, 2003).

5.1.1 Open communication

Applying the term *process* to communication means that it is an ongoing event. In our social interaction with others, we communicating. Communicate, therefore, is the process whereby we attempt to transmit our thoughts, ideas, wishes, or emotions to others in a climate of transparency, that is, open communication.

Maintaining open communication is one of the keys to creating a welcoming and healthy environment. A project manager should be honest and fair, and provide concrete, constructive feedback. Sharing relevant information and maintaining open communication help create a sense of trust. The more information people are given, the greater the likelihood that they will perceive the environment as open and the project manager as someone they can trust. Moreover, making decisions openly and encouraging feedback from project team members help to create a sense of buy-in, ownership, and community, which in turn lead to improved leadership.

Open communication has been ranked as one of the most important reasons employees reported for taking jobs in project management (*Computer Weekly*, 2004). Project personnel want to know what is going on in the workplace; by telling them, managers provide motivation. A question for project managers is: How often do you take the time to do it? Project managers will get what they reward in the workplace. Studies reinforce the notion that job satisfaction and work motivation are helped by the quality of communication within the organization. There is a need to listen to employees' views, establish dialogue, develop consensus, act on agreed ideas, and delegate responsibility. Joint consultation is used within some organizations; it improves employee relations and fills in the gap left by some management practices, while creating good working relationships between management and employees. Involvement in problem solving provides employees with an opportunity to contribute directly to the achievement of the organizational and project goals.

5.1.2 Team communication

As discussed in Chapter 2, multidisciplinary project teams are the vehicle through which many of the activities associated with project management are accomplished. Any aspiring project manager is expected to function effectively on multidisciplinary teams. A key attribute of multidisciplinary team participation is intrateam communication. This is a process through which team members communicate with one another. It is made up of the communication strategies and styles of each member of the team. Like interpersonal communication skills, a team can improve its intrateam communication skills through knowledge, practice, feedback, and reflection on the exchange of ideas and information.

Within multidisciplinary project teams, the exchange of ideas and information is the essence of how people interface with one another with regard to sharing ideas and working effectively together. Faulty communication lies at the heart of conflict, which may lead to ineffective communication. As pointed out in Table 4.2, over 90% of conflicts are attributed to faulty communication between sender and receiver. However, when individuals and team members think about and choose their communication styles, then opportunities for miscommunication and the resulting conflict are reduced. How you communicate impacts how others communicate within your team. How your team members communicate impacts the "thinking environment" of your team and its productivity and efficiency. Better understanding of the communication process, how we communicate, potential pitfalls in communication, and improving communication skills will help project teams improve their performance and help team members improve their interpersonal communication skills.

5.1.3 Network communication

Project managers are expected to operate and communicate at many levels within the organization and deal with many stakeholder groups. As leaders, project managers have an obligation to create communities that serve the project and its stakeholders. One way to create a sense of "project community" is to help build informal networks. Several means of building these networks include:

- Regular project- or senior management-hosted social events.
- Department-sponsored quarterly lunches for stakeholder groups. These could vary each quarter so that project team members have a chance to interact with different groups of colleagues.
- Invitations to lunch by the Department Director for young team members to demonstrate goodwill.
- Monthly dinner outings for clients and key stakeholders.

Research into the benefits of social networks reveal that:

- Teams with better access to other teams inside and outside the organization finished their tasks more productively.

- Teams with better connections discovered and transferred the knowledge they needed within the organization.
- Managers with "better connections" (inside and outside the organization) spotted and developed more opportunities for their departments or organizations.
- Project managers with better network connections were more successful in reaching project goals within time and financial parameters.

Research shows that most project communities start as small emergent clusters organized around common interests or goals. Usually these clusters are isolated from each other. They are very small groups of 1–5 people or organizations that have connected out of necessity. Many of these small clusters are found in underdeveloped communities. If these clusters do not organize further, the community structure remains weak and under-producing. Without an active leader who takes responsibility for building a network, spontaneous connections between groups emerge very slowly, or not at all. We call this network leadership role a *"network weaver"*. Instead of allowing these small clusters to drift in the hope of making a lucky connection, the weaver actively creates new interactions between the clusters. Through this activity, useful community structures emerge (Krebs and Holly, 2002).

5.2 Creating a communications strategy

All communication is associated with initiating some form of action or behaviour. Communication is generally one of three types (Table 5.1). At its simplest level, top-down communication is used to instruct, control, and direct impersonally. Top-down communication is commonly associated with hierarchically structured, centrally driven organizations in which decisions are taken without too much consultation at the lower operating levels within the hierarchy. Feedback is not a requirement though team briefings are usually undertaken by middle managers.

In contrast to top-down communication, the purpose of two-way communication is to create the conditions under which people freely contribute more to the achievement of the goals of the organization. Two-way communication is associated with participatory styles of management, best practice, and the alignment of project goals and personal goals.

Table 5.1 Types of communication

Type of communication	Explanation
Downward communication	The process is management owned and controlled and is used to pass information down through the organization
Downward and upward communication	A two-way flow of information is exchanged between management and operating staff – ownership of the process is sometimes shared
Downward, upward, and lateral communication	There is a free exchange of information across the organization

Three-way communication that is downward, upward, and lateral are a feature of "project organizations" in which people are encouraged to cross barriers to get the information they need to do the job.

In creating a communication strategy for project management, it is sensible to ask who in the organization (and outside the organization) will be affected by the project. It could be argued that communication delivers most when everybody owns it. Deciding who has a stake in the project and the communication process falls invariably to the project manager. The more complex the project, the more you need to involve stakeholders.

Catering for different stakeholders involves developing good communication channels between the project and its stakeholder community. One method of achieving this is through the appointment of a communication liaison officer. This person acts as a focal point for channelling information from and to the project identifying and administering communication training and preparing project and stakeholder reports.

5.2.1 Communicating with project stakeholders

During the lifecycle of a project, it is highly unlikely that the expectations of all stakeholders will be met. Therefore, the project manager must somehow ascertain which stakeholders should be satisfied. Since stakeholders have the ability to positively or negatively influence the outcome of a project, communicating and integrating stakeholder expectations is essential. Specific organizational and project strategies used to integrate stakeholders will differ, depending on the issue and the group's potential to cooperate or threaten the project.

In developing communication strategy, the project manager needs to consider that each stakeholder has the ability to both threaten and cooperate, the objective of the strategy must be to reduce the threatening element and increase the cooperative behaviour of the stakeholder. It is important to realize that the stakeholders' potential to act and their willingness to act are not directly related. Therefore, when looking at communication or involvement strategies, it is important to examine not only strategies addressing stakeholders who are positively disposed towards a project but those who are negatively disposed towards a project as well. Some strategies may only be appropriate for a stakeholder with a specific disposition towards the project, that is, positive or negative. In other cases, a given strategy may be appropriate for either type of stakeholder, i.e. both. As shown in Table 5.2, there are several different strategies for different types of stakeholders. Each strategy is not mutually exclusive; some are appropriate for more than one type of stakeholder group.

In cases where stakeholders cannot be communicated with, due to their negative disposition towards the project, alternative communication strategies should be developed. Such strategies may attempt to change the stakeholder group's disposition or minimize its negativity. Strategies to undertake this change may require the project to use bridging stakeholders to "communicate" on behalf of the project with these negatively disposed stakeholders. In cases where stakeholders' expectations cannot be met or changed, the firm will at least be able to develop contingency plans to minimize any potential harm (Polonsky, 1995).

5.2.2 Communication participation and collaboration

As discussed in Chapter 3, many project decision-making processes include a stakeholder participation stage. In this stage, project managers disseminate information and request the stakeholder feedback and input. This may be accomplished through meetings, the submittal of written comment, or various sorts of forums and other outreach activities. Following this stage, the

Table 5.2 Stakeholder communication strategies

Type	View	Strategy
Mixed blessing	These stakeholders are extremely important, for they have the ability to cooperate with the project or threaten the achievement of the project objectives	One appropriate strategy for mixed-blessing stakeholders is to integrate them into the project strategy development process. This will ensure that the objectives of the stakeholders are included in the strategy as it is formed and thus will not require a later "redevelopment" of strategy
Supportive	These stakeholders have the ability to be cooperative with the project, but have little ability to threaten its activities	This group may require extremely innovative strategies to be developed in order to diffuse negatively disposed stakeholders within the group
Nonsupportive	These stakeholders have the ability to threaten the project activities, but have little ability to cooperate with the project organization. Governmental bodies are often considered to be nonsupportive stakeholders	Use collaborative strategies, for example, Joint Project Boards. Using a collaborative strategy minimizes the potential of threatening behaviour form and increases its cooperative behaviour
Marginal	These stakeholders have little ability to threaten the project activities or to cooperate with the project. This group may have little interest in the project activities at a given point in time	Interest may change over time and therefore the potential for cooperation or threat may change. Under such circumstances a collaborative strategy minimizes the potential for threatening behaviour
Bridging	One definition of the term *bridging stakeholders* is all groups who forward their own ends as well as to serve as links between other stakeholders	One positive strategy would be to have open communication channels with the bridging stakeholders. This would allow projects to "influence" the bridging group's actions and therefore indirectly affect the "influenced" groups' expectations or behaviour towards the project itself

(Source: McManus 2002; adapted from Polonsky, 1995).

project manager considers the stakeholder input and weaves the pertinent information into their decisions.

While this approach ensures an opportunity for stakeholder review and comment, there is little opportunity for true communication or a stakeholder's ability to effectively influence decision makers. A collaborative process is not the same as a stakeholder involvement process. In a collaborative process, stakeholders work directly with project managers to develop agreements or recommendations on project policy issues. Although both activities share the goals of informing the stakeholder community, there are significant differences in seeking meaningful input and building a basis for a decision. The summary (Table 5.3) outlines key differences between stakeholder involvement and a collaborative process.

5.3 Communication skills

Communication involves both receiving and sending messages (see Table 5.4). For the purpose of management, it is important to give thoughtful consideration on how to accomplish each task most effectively. In this respect what management is looking for is judgement, the ability to communicate (which means listening as well as speaking), humaneneas and concern, openness of mind, and the ability to concentrate and that hard for a goal that the individual has to buy into.

It has been said "that we are born with one mouth and two ears, so we should listen twice as much as we talk." Listening is the

Table 5.3 Comparison of participation and collaborative communication process

Communication scenario	Participation	Collaboration process
Stakeholders	Act as advocates (independent)	Are decision makers (interactive)
Objectives	Hear from all stakeholders	Search for single voice
Approach	Stakeholders take sides	Stakeholders focus on interests
Activity	Make representation	Find common ground
Interaction	Stakeholders act alone	Stakeholders interact with each other
Negotiation	Behind close doors	Open sessions
Outcome	Many inputs, but single decision	One decision or recommendation
Timing	Usually prescribed	Stakeholders decide

Table 5.4 Simple communication model

Communication	Send	Receive
Verbal	Verbal indicators you give to others	Verbal indicators that others give to you
Visual	Behavioural indicators, such as hand movements that you give to others	Behavioural indicators others give to you

(Source of points 1–5 in Section 5.6.1, Wiegers and Rothman, 2001; McManus and Wood-Harper, 2003, pp. 32–33).

most critical communication skill. Effective listening ensures that the message being received is the message that was intended to be sent. Done correctly, listening is anything but a passive process; it requires focussed attention and a discerning mind. Listening even involves speaking; restating to the speaker what you heard and asking questions to get issues clarified. To be effective, listening skills must be actively cultivated. It is argued that leaders have a high propensity for listening to their staff needs.

Sir John Harvey Jones, writing on leadership, comments that communication is a continual process in which catalytic interventions take place. He makes a point that many problems associated with industrial relation matters stem from misunderstandings in communication and the lack of accurate and fast communication. Such problems are quite often about issues, which themselves are not of great importance but are the fuse that allows dissatisfaction to boil over.

Experienced project managers will be familiar with what Harvey Jones calls reverse-catalytic reactions, in other words, a small unrewarded action that worsens an already bad situation in a dramatic way; the extra turn down on the relief value that finally causes an entire situation top explode; the inadvertent pushing of something one step too fare that brings the whole situation to the boil. How many times have you found yourself wishing you had never opened your mouth; feeling certain that had you not said anything everyone would be better off? Well, the truth is, it is generally necessary to open your mouth to communicate. Yet it is wise to do so with prudence, to ensure that the words that are spoken do not unnecessarily contribute to an already poor communication situation.

When trying to promote understanding and avert differences, there are two primary reasons to communicate:

1. To gain a clearer understanding of the other party's views and interests
2. To effectively communicate your views and interests.

A certain amount of skill is involved in doing each of these things effectively. It is best to keep these two tasks separate. First listen to the other person's story, asking questions only as necessary to get a more complete understanding of it. Wait until they have completely finished telling the story before offering your perspective. When listening to the story, use the following examples to help ensure that the other party will feel they are being heard. For example:

- Focus on the message
- Indicate when you are making assumptions and the basis for them
- Allow the other party to express their experience and perspective. When your perspective differs from theirs, refrain from implying that they are wrong. Simply state your experience and leave it at that.
- *Maintain credibility*. Do not say anything that you know is not true; do not make promises that you cannot keep.
- Make an effort to avoid speculation.
- *Enhance legitimacy*. Do not act in ways you would not want others to act towards you.

Although communication, to some degree, is a science, it is also an art form and in essence can only be derived from a real understanding of people (which can take a life time to achieve). In many respects, the real art and substance of communication cannot be taught within a business school environment, but it is a subject which project managers should address themselves to.

5.4 Communication planning

Project managers who have a high quotient of emotional intelligence invariably enjoy continuously excellent internal communication, which they view as strategically important. At its best, good internal communication helps the project manager to realize the full potential of the people under his or her domain by managing their fears, wants, and needs.

Encouraging positive behaviour in communication helps the project manager to deliver on time and increases performance and client satisfaction. Like most things in life, however, success needs to be planned for – failing to plan means planning to fail.

As stated earlier, communication delivers most when everybody owns it. Ownership is about taking proactive action and responsibility when the need arises. Although ownership plays a key role in communications planning in many respects, it is a collaborative process that involves multiple stakeholders. Successful use of collaborative processes in communications planning requires a change in ethic (see also Chapter 6) that looks for long-term solutions that are carefully arrived at after consultation with stakeholders, not quick, top-down answers.

Communications planning with the proper investment of time, resources, and collaboration becomes both a problem solving process and a learning process. Perhaps the greatest payoff that comes from successful use of communication planning is the groundwork that is laid for future cooperation within the project community.

5.4.1 The planning process

Communications planning generally involves four phases. Within each phase, the participants will normally work through several tasks to accomplish the specific objectives (Figure 5.1). The phases are:

1. Assessment of needs
2. Formulate plan
3. Implementation plan
4. Feedback.

5.4.1.1 Phase 1: assessment

The assessment phase is a critical first step in determining the scope of communications planning. The objectives of an assessment are to identify key communications issues and which stakeholders will be affected and those that will play a vital role in the project. Conducting an assessment provides valuable information and assists the management team to determine which collaborative agreement-seeking processes are appropriate for the issues at hand. The assessment phase should include data and information on:

- Degree of disclosure (if you wish to communicate in advance make sure that what is fixed and what is open disclosure) is made clear

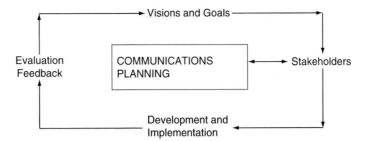

Figure 5.1
Overview communications planning.

- The message (clear common messages, avoid doubts and reactions that can result from minor variations)
- The content (put forward clear reasons for the objectives you set; declare a positive aim around which staff can unify and be energized)
- The timing (communicate as far ahead as possible and give time for staff and other stakeholders to absorb the significance of the message and come to terms with changes that are being proposed).

The people (ensure that the message is given in the right way, at the right level, and in the right language).

5.4.1.2 Phase 2: formulate plan

Once the assessment phase is concluded, the next task is to assimilate the findings from the assessment and recommend a suitable course of action. There is no precise formula for determining the right communication plan or whether it is likely to succeed or hit the right mark. However, there are a number of key indicators that contribute to what may be considered best practice.

- Keep the process simple
- Know your audience
- Maintain an overview of the vision
- Define clear roles and responsibilities
- Set concise deliverables
- Perform validations at appropriate intervals
- Use appropriate validation criteria
- Represent your vision by words and deeds.

5.4.1.3 Phase 3: implementation

Once an agreement is reached as to the content of the plan, the work of implementation and monitoring begins. Although the

111

process often creates a great deal of good will, the progress can be wiped out by a lack of attention to detail following agreement to implement the plan. During the implantation phase, the project manager should support the actions of the implementers and ensure that all actions are concluded in line with the agreed deliverables. The project manager should have regular meetings with stakeholders and progress should be monitored at frequent intervals. Those involved in the implantation phase have an opportunity and obligation to:

- Help refine the process for monitoring and evaluation
- Help stakeholders to "link" major issues to the formal decision-making process
- Bring together stakeholders if subsequent disagreements emerge during implementation
- Give feedback.

Although a communications plan will have set out the vision for describing what should be accomplished and to what extent, a vast gap will remain between the vision and the actual realities of what happens postimplementation. Obviously, there is no way to guarantee that the official decisions taken will be completely consistent with the original plan that was implemented. That fact should be acknowledged. However, the following measures can be taken during the communication process to improve the chances that the project managers' actions are consistent with the vision:

- Make every effort to ensure that feedback mechanisms are in place
- Make every effort to ensure that you promptly deal with any communication issues from whatever source
- Make every effort to ensure that you evaluate information from stakeholder feedback sessions
- Make every effort to ensure that working documents are updated and are fit for purpose
- Make every effort to ensure that measures of performance accurately reflect the current situation
- Make every effort to ensure that your stakeholders are happy with what you are doing.

5.5 Barriers to communication

In my experience, good communication practice is easier to achieve in organizations that have mature processes and methodologies such as PRINCE or (People-Capability Maturity

Model) P-CMM. The software industry is taken as an example where communication between stakeholders is cited as a causal factor for poor delivery of projects and failure to provide what the customer wants. While the extent of these problems has probably been embellished, major problems do occur in communication and in the management of stakeholder relationships.

One weakness is that communications processes do deteriorate with time and are seldom robust enough to deliver the vision that project managers would like. As alluded to in the previous section, a common weakness is to confuse information giving with communication receiving (understanding, acting upon exchanging information). Insufficient regard and time is given to understanding this distinction, and to the tools and skills needed to encourage effective communication.

In my career, I was once a Delivery Director on a project that was experiencing difficulties – my objectives were rebuilding the project team and gaining the trust of the client. The relationship with the client was in some difficulty, trust was low, and there was a strong combative atmosphere among the project manager, client, and their senior stakeholders. At the root of the problem was vision and expectations, in that neither was being met. This had led to a series of confrontations in which the project manager's reputation had been seriously damaged, but he still had the support of his team.

Looking around the room at "my" first encounter with the client and project manager, I saw two highly motivated and experienced IT professionals. The issue was that each perceived to be in the right and was using tactics that were counterproductive to the project. Each person was sending and receiving information that was fuelling individual behaviour.

All too often IT professionals see themselves at the top of their game and can become arrogant in their assessment of clients and users and this leads to confrontation. Another failing is seeing the client as a colleague who we can manipulate and treat according to our own needs and desires. We might even be tempted to lie or provide false information in order to keep a difficult situation under our control. Painful as these observations might be they nonetheless exist in even the best of organizations.

The fact is how you perceive people and behave towards them is important; for example, if the client is sending you negative e-mails it generally means you have not been managing the relationship correctly. In the world of projects, stakeholders have to be managed and above all else we have to manage their expectations. One objective of stakeholder management is to never end up with a surprised client. A surprised client is seldom a happy one. When this occurs, it generally means that we have lost focus and allowed other issues to get in the way of communicating to our client (or key stakeholders) in a direct and timely way. By the avoiding of communication obligations some believe that given time the situation may go away – however, the reality is that it usually gets worse. Good leaders and project managers will agree that it makes good sense. The problem is that the skills do not reach deep enough into the organization and the day-to-day behaviour of people. A belief prevails that communication is something project managers just do, without the need for training in communication skills.

Today's project managers (and their staff) need to be immersed in the skills and behaviour of stakeholders rather than users. Acquiring communication skills is fundamental to the successful delivery of projects. Wrong or poorly delivered messages impact all and can have severe consequences. Good communication helps create a positive environment by bringing about an alignment and satisfaction of interests – matching what stakeholders want for their projects and what their stakeholders want out of their communication experiences is important because good communication costs relatively little, and may in the long run save millions of pounds (or dollars). On the other hand, poor communication costs a great deal, causing pain, stress and confrontation at all levels, lowering morale and team performance, and damaging relationships and health sometimes irretrievably. Although not exhaustive, some of the following characteristics can be barriers to effective communication:

- A history of individual or organizational communication
- Lack of consensus among stakeholders
- Lack of endorsement on policy
- Lack of compromise
- Lack of empathy
- Failure to recognize the strategic importance and value of communication
- Behaviour that is inconsistent with communication policy and practice
- Unsympathetic managers, clients, or stakeholders
- Rigid or enforced behaviour
- Rigid thinking
- Rigid or uncompromising language.

5.6 Communication feedback and audits

As discussed in Section 5.5, the undermining and failure of many projects is to some extent associated with poor communication. Any communication process should have a feedback mechanism, which acts as a means of highlighting discrepancies between what was envisioned and what actually occurs.

Some project managers have a very clear approach to feedback mechanisms in that people should read the communications plan and know what information is required of them and when and in what format, and if they fail to provide it accurately, they are penalized in some way.

A favourite mechanism adopted by many project managers is to adopt a system of cross-checking the information that is given (this is certainly appropriate if verbal communication is the means of feedback). This is necessary at times, but can be counterproductive. If individuals know that their information is being cross-checked, they may not put a great deal of effort into providing accurate answers to questions asked of them. The person may also feel angered at the apparent lack of trust and may go out of the way to undermine your efforts. Another favoured approach is to ask for feedback in writing. Whilst this is useful and a legitimate way of obtaining information, it can have the same effect as cross-checking with the added one that people will not usually be willing to give as much in writing as face-to-face.

It may prove more productive, after being given some information, to send the giver a memo (e-mail), which summarizes what was said or agreed. This serves to check the accuracy of communication and to remind them of any commitments they may have given or made. Project managers tend to support the view that the most important part of receiving and giving feedback involves keeping minutes of actions. Many project managers receive feedback on activities that may have occurred some time ago. Feedback should be received as soon as possible after the event had taken place. Maintaining an audit trail of events is useful and allows for transparency within the process and enables good governance (a point we will discuss in Chapter 6).

5.6.1 Communication audits

Although there are no hard-and-fast rules on when to undertake a communications audit, it is generally accepted that such audits should take place at frequent intervals (say, once a month or at the end of a stage of a project), the project manger, however, may choose to exercise his or her authority and leadership and undertake reviews at the request of the client or key stakeholders.

A communications audit can succeed only in a neutral, nonaccusatory environment. Honest and open communication is essential. If a project has been difficult or unsuccessful, some venting is to be expected; however, the facilitator must limit that venting and channel it in a constructive direction. Make sure your retrospectives do not turn into witch hunts. The retrospective must emphasize guilt-free learning from the shared project experience. Let us look at some audit critical success factors.

5.6.1.1 Define your objectives

As the project manager, you should identify your objectives for the communications audit and the specific project aspects on which it should focus, along with identifying the potential beneficiaries of the activity: Who will come out ahead if the information gathered during the communications audit guides some constructive process changes? Also, think about who might look bad if the root causes of problems are revealed. Remember, you are not looking for scapegoats, but you need to understand what really happened and why.

5.6.1.2 Use a skilled and impartial facilitator

It is not realistic to expect project managers to objectively facilitate a communications audit. They might have a particular axe to grind or want to protect their own reputation. Some project managers might unconsciously impede participation despite their good intentions. Other participants can be intimidated into silence on important points, or managers might put their own spin on certain issues.

To avoid these problems, invite an experienced, neutral facilitator from outside the project team to lead the communications audit. The facilitator's prime objective is to make the communications audit succeed by surfacing the critical issues in a constructive, learning environment. Consider having someone who is not an active participant in the communications audit act as scribe to record the issues generated.

5.6.1.3 Engage the right participants

Of course, the essential participants are all the project team members. Management representatives are invited to the communications audit only if they were actually members of the project team. However, you should provide a summary of lessons learned to senior management or to other managers in the company who could benefit from the information.

Some teams might be too busy, too large, or too geographically separated for all team members to participate in a communications audit concurrently. In such a case, select representatives of the various functional areas that were involved in the project. If a large project was subdivided into multiple subprojects, each should perform its own communications audit. Delegates from each subproject can then participate in a higher-level communications audit at the overall project level.

When people who we believe have key insights claim they are too busy to participate, we ask them if they think everything went well on the project. Generally, they have some important observations and constructive suggestions. We then help those people balance their current time demands against the need to hear their input on the previous project.

If the project involved multiple groups who blame each other for the project's problems or who refuse to sit down together to explore their common issues, you might begin by discussing the friction points between the groups. Chances are good that you will uncover important project issues. If the groups cannot get along in the communications audit, they probably had clashed during the project, too. The communications audit might address what needs to change for those groups to collaborate more effectively next time.

5.6.1.4 Prepare the participants

If the participants are not accustomed to communications audits, and if the project studied had serious problems, an invitation to a communications audit can stimulate fear, confusion, or resistance. Some participants might be sick with anxiety, while others will be eager to let the accusations fly. Provide information and reassurance to the participants through the invitation material and during "sales calls" made on team leaders and key participants. Describe the process in advance and establish an appropriately constructive mindset by emphasizing that this is a future-oriented and process-improvement activity.

5.6.1.5 Focus on the facts

A communications audit should address the processes and outcomes of the project, not the participants' personalities or mistakes. The facilitator has to ensure that the participants do not blame or placate others by concentrating on what actually happened. However, people often experience events in different ways. Understanding the different interpretations can release hard feelings and provide the opportunity for new insights.

5.6.1.6 Write an action plan

For maximum benefit, any weaknesses identified during the audit process should be first discussed with the project manager (and then with the team and key stakeholders). If the audit was undertaken at the request of the client, it should be discussed in the presence of the project manager.

Experienced project managers know that any weakness found during the audit will have repercussions (some may be major). After the audit is concluded take a while to reflect, do not try to tackle any issues that may have been identified immediately. Choose issues from a priority perspective. Write an action plan that describes how you will address the issues – obtain support from those who can repair or fix the situation. State who will take responsibility for each action and list any follow up action that will be taken and follow through. At the next audit, check whether the proposed actions resulted in the desired outcomes – an action plan that does not lead to a successful outcome is useless.

5.7 Chapter summary – 10 key points

The most important points to take away from this chapter are:

1. Result-orientated leaders (and project managers) often see themselves as catalysts or interventionists. They expect to achieve a great deal, but know they can do little without the efforts of others.
2. Sharing relevant information and maintaining open communication help create a sense of trust. The more information people are given, the greater the likelihood that they will perceive the environment as open and the project manager as someone they can trust.
3. Studies reinforce the notion that job satisfaction and work motivation are helped by the quality of communication within the organization.
4. Like interpersonal communication skills, a team can improve its intrateam communication skills through knowledge, practice, feedback, and reflection on the exchange of ideas and information.

5. In contrast to top-down communication, the purpose of two-way communication is to create the conditions under which people freely contribute more to the achievement of the goals of the organization.

6. A collaborative process is not the same as a stakeholder involvement process. In a collaborative process, stakeholders work directly with project managers to develop agreements or recommendations on project policy issues. Although both activities share the goals of informing the stakeholder community, seeking meaningful input and building a basis for a decision, there are significant differences.

7. Catering for different stakeholders involves developing good communication channels between the project and its stakeholder community.

8. Although communication is to some degree a science, it is also an art form and in essence can only be derived from a real understanding of people (which can take a life time to achieve).

9. Communications planning with the proper investment of time, resources, and collaboration becomes both a problem-solving process and a learning process. Perhaps the greatest payoff that comes from successful use of communication planning is the groundwork that is laid for future cooperation within the project community.

10. A communications audit can succeed only in a neutral, nonaccusatory environment. Honest and open communication is essential. If a project has been difficult or unsuccessful, some venting is to be expected; however, the facilitator must limit that venting and channel it in a constructive direction.

5.8 Next chapter

In the next chapter, we will explore some of the issues associated with ethics and leadership. We will also look at the legal and governance frameworks that surround project managers and how the leader is expected to behave and deal with the complexities of decision making in some areas of governance.

Chapter references

Computer Weekly Archives, for 2004, Issues in communication and leadership.

Krebs, V. and J. Holly (2002) Building Sustainable Communities through Network Building. OrgNet.com Publication.

McManus, J. (2002) The influence of stakeholder values: project management. Management Services, 8–15.

McManus, J. and T. Wood-Harper (2003) Information Systems Project Management: Methods, Tools and Techniques. Upper Saddle River, NJ, Pearson Education (Prentice Hall).

Polonsky, M.J. (1995) Incorporating the natural environment in corporate strategy: a stakeholder approach. The Journal of Business Strategies, 12(2).

Turner, J.R. (1993) The Handbook of Project Management. London, McGraw-Hill.

Wiegers K.E. and J. Rothman, Looking back, looking ahead in McManus, J. & Wood-Harper, T., (2003), Information Systems Project Management: Methods, Tools and Techniques, Pearson Education, Prentice Hall.

Further reading

Ettinger, B. and E. Perfetto (2001) Communication for the Workplace: An Integrated Language Approach. Upper Saddle River, NJ, Prentice Hall, Inc.

James, T.R. (1992) STOP, GO, and the state of the art in proposal writing. IEEE Transactions in Professional Communication 35, 143–155.

Locker, K. (1999) Business and Administrative Communication. Chicago, IL, Irwin Professional Publications.

Margerison, C. (1990) If Only I Had Said: Conversation Control Skills for Managers. Mercury Business Books.

Thill, J. and C. Bovee (1999) Business Communication Today (6th edition). Upper Saddle River, NJ, Prentice Hall.

Ethics and Governance: A Leadership Perspective

6.1 Ethics and leadership

The term *ethics* may be described as the moral considerations of the activities of an organization or a system, or code of conduct that is based on universal moral duties and obligations that indicate how one should behave. It deals with the ability to distinguish good from evil, right from wrong, and propriety from impropriety. The keywords here are moral duties and obligations. It has been suggested that ethical leadership includes two pillars: the moral person and the moral manager.

Project managers often fail to recognize the importance of stakeholder perceptions and the development of their own ethical leadership. Many believe being an ethical person and making sound ethical decisions is enough; furthermore, they believe good project managers are by definition ethical leaders. However, this is not necessarily true. Fulton defines ethics as:

> the dilemma we all face every day, having to choose between action that benefits our own self-interest, and action that addresses our obligation to one another: our self-interest, including the need to profit from our dealings with others, versus the "moral" perspective, the social contract that binds us to others (1998).

The project manager as a moral person is characterized in terms of individual traits; as a moral manager, he is thought of as conveying an ethics message that others take notice of in their views and behaviours. The basis of ethical leadership is being an ethical person. Individuals must think of you as having certain traits, engaging in certain kinds of behaviours, and making decisions based upon ethical principles. Moreover, this ethical self must be authentic. Ethical traits relating to trust include moral order, integrity, honesty, fairness, and fulfilment of obligations.

While traits are clearly important, behaviours are equally important. Behaviours include doing the right thing, showing concern for people and treating people right, being open and communicative, and demonstrating morality in one's personal life. In the decision-making role, project managers should have a set of ethical values and principles; they should aim to be unbiased and reasonable. A project manager's decisions should look beyond the balance sheet; the "moral person" represents the essence of the ethical manager.

Project managers need to recognize the importance of proactively putting ethics at the forefront of their agenda; they need to make the ethical dimension of their leadership explicit and salient to their subordinates. One can become an ethical project manager by serving as a visible and vocal role model for ethical conduct, and ethical management can be achieved using a reward system holding all employees accountable to ethical standards.

The ethical project manager as a leader must be both a moral person and a moral manager. This manager is both a substantively ethical person and a leader who makes ethics and values a prominent part of the leadership agenda. Ethical management is good for the project and avoids issues, for example, legal, later and contributes to team commitment and satisfaction. The project manager must also find ways to focus the stakeholders' attention on ethics and values and to instil the project management team with the principles to guide their actions. An ethical project manager and leader is important more than ever in today's project management and market climate (Floyd and McManus, 2004).

It could be argued that no current methodology of project management considers ethical issues and their impact on stakeholder and client relationships. In the last decade, project management had a history of ethical dilemmas (no more so than in the computing industry). Consequences of unethical behaviour in the computing industry have led to the loss of thousands of jobs, stress, suicide, lawsuits, bankruptcy, and loss of reputation.

Recent corporate scandals such as Enron have placed ethics and governance high on the public agenda. Major project work undertaken by large IT service providers (and their project managers) on behalf of the UK Government such as the NHS National Programme for IT (NPfIT) is now scrutinized more than ever by the media, the tax-paying public, and Government audit teams. Project leadership, as explained in the previous chapters, involves balancing many issues of a political, economic, social, and commercial nature. Although few managers would go on record, amongst my former peer managers there is a strong belief that ethics is irrelevant because it gets in the way of achievement, and when you need back up people run for cover.

Overcoming apathy to ethical considerations is one task the project manager "must" take lead in. One of the key characteristics of ethical leadership is that of being a role model through visible action. Most leadership positions in management, involve removal of "coal-face operations" from the day-to-day activities. Senior executives rarely, if ever, deal face-to-face with middle-ranking project managers or junior staff. It is the time-old problem of decision makers being divorced from the "front line" entanglements, which causes policies to be divorced from reality. Also, what often passes for professionalism in management is usually simply a cover to maintain the "great divide" between management and the rest of the organization.

Understanding the organization and the extent and nature of the ethical problem is the leader's first step towards meeting this challenge. But it may be just as important to understand why it matters. There is substantial evidence that fairness is indispensable to institutional ethics and leadership success, contributing to effectiveness in measurable ways. The leadership imperative, then, is to translate this understanding into action by doing the hard work of building relationships based on consistently demonstrated ethical trust. As a former colleague of mine puts it:

> *I am me. Respect me for what I am rather than what you want me to be, and I will do the same for you. I will be open and honest with you and I expect the same in return. Betray that trust and I will simply move to where it is not betrayed. This behaviour defines the new connected world, its markets and its servants.*
>
> *Mel Earp, Technical Director, Sema Group*

6.2 Ethics and moral rules of behaviour

Going back to our discussion on project stakeholders in Section 5.2, stakeholders tend to have high expectations of project managers and their employing organizations. In this respect, how one behaves and acts is a reflection of the organization. Behaviour is important because stakeholder perceptions and ethical outcomes are positive when they see ethical behaviours in practice.

Stakeholder have different legal, economic, and social relationship to a particular business project, sometimes a general stakeholder identification approach may not be too helpful in defining and explaining specific ethical obligations of managers to their stakeholders. The right model developed by Gert is a useful one to identify relevant project stakeholders. Once the stakeholders are identified, one can itemize the specific obligations owed by the managers to each of them. Gert (1998) gives 10 basic moral rules:

1. Do not kill
2. Do not cause pain
3. Do not disable
4. Do not deprive of freedom
5. Do not deprive of pleasure
6. Do not deceive
7. Do not cheat
8. Do keep your promises
9. Obey the law
10. Do your duty.

These rules carry with them a corresponding set of rights such as the right to liberty, physical security, personal liberty, free speech, and property. Using this model a preliminary identification of project stakeholders is accomplished by listing each of these rules and rights, and examining the project goals to see who is affected and how they may be affected. Some of the rights and obligations identified when following this method may be in conflict and it will become necessary to prioritize how these rights are addressed and which of them can, within the bounds of the principles above, be addressed (Rogerson and Gotterbarn, 1998).

One of the ways to help prioritize the ethical obligations within a project is to determine what actions are necessary to satisfy the perceived obligation and evaluate those actions in terms of whether they are morally required, morally wrong, or are merely morally permissible (Floyd and McManus, 2004).

6.2.1 Ideology and ethics

As many academics have noted, many business organizations are run on the basis of ideology more than anything else. An ideology is *a set of beliefs or assumptions about the proper state of things, particularly with respect to the moral order and political arrangements which serve to shape one's position on issues* (Hornum and Stavish, 1978). Conflicting ideologies usually influence managers by creating goal ambiguity. An ideology also refers to a belief in something as true that is actually false, or at the base of it, containing a falsehood. Ideologies survive by putting a positive spin on something negative. According to Emile Durkheim, ideologies always rest on a lie. They are the opposite of the word *institution* because anything that reaches the level of social institution must rest on a kernel of truth. Ideologies require myths to survive.

In business organizations, ethics is to some degree considered a management discipline (in which leaders are expected to play a part) that may be interpreted as a value system. It has been observed by mcNamara that myths flourish in relation to ethics; some of them emerge from the confusion about ethics generally and others arise from simplistic view of ethical dilemmas (Table 6.1).

Table 6.1 Ten myths about ethics

Myth	Truth
1. Business ethics is more a matter of religion than management	It is managing values and conflict
2. Our employees are ethical so we do not need to pay attention to business ethics	Most of the ethical dilemmas faced by managers in the the workplace are highly complex and when presented with complex ethical dilemmas, most people realize there is a wide "grey area" when trying to apply ethical principles
3. Business ethics is a discipline best led by philosophers, academics, and theologians	Ethics is a management discipline with a programmatic approach that includes several practical tools
4. Business ethics is superfluous; it only asserts the obvious that is do good	The value of a code of ethics to an organization is its priority and focus regarding certain ethical values in that workplace
5. Business ethics is a matter of the good guys preaching to the bad guys	Managing ethics in the workplace includes all of us working together to help each other remain ethical and to work through confusing and stressful ethical dilemmas
6. Business ethics is the new policeman on the block	Business ethics was written about even 2000 years ago, at least since Cicero wrote about the topic in his *On Duties*. Business ethics has got more attention recently because of the social responsibility movement (1960s)

Table 6.1 (Continued)

Myth	Truth
7. Ethics cannot be managed	Actually, ethics is always "managed" – but, too often, indirectly. For example, the behaviour of the organization's founder or current leader is a strong moral influence or directive if you will, on behaviour or employees in the workplace. Strategic priorities (profit maximization, expanding market share, cutting costs, etc.) can be very strong influences on morality. Laws, regulations and rules directly influence behaviours to be more ethical
8. Business ethics and social responsibility are the same thing	The social responsibility movement is one aspect of the overall discipline of business ethics. Writings about social responsibility often do not address practical matters of managing ethics in the workplace
9. Our organization is not in trouble with the law, so we are ethical	One can often be unethical, yet operate within the limits of the law, e.g. withhold information from superiors, fudge on budgets, constantly complain about others, etc. However, breaking the law often starts with unethical behaviour that has gone unnoticed
10. Managing ethics in the workplace has little practical relevance	Managing ethics in the workplace involves identifying and prioritizing values to guide behaviours in the organization, and establishing associated policies and procedures to ensure that those behaviours are conducted.

Source: adapted from the work of McNamara and reproduced with permission.

For leaders and project managers, ethics involves learning what is right and what is wrong, and then doing the right thing. Even so, the right thing is not nearly as basic as conveyed since it may depend on the situation. Values that guide behaviour are moral values such as respect, honesty, and fairness. Statements around how these values are applied are sometimes referred to as moral principles. Consideration of ethics in project leadership will ensure that when a problem arises, or confusion exists, project managers will have a sense of right and wrong.

6.3 Ethics and the communication interface

Communication is now considered an individual and social necessity of such fundamental importance that it is seen as a universal human right. Communication as a human right encompasses the traditional freedoms of expression, of the right to seek, receive, and impart information. But it adds to these freedoms, both for individuals and society, a new concept, namely that of access, participation, and two-way flow. The right to receive information and the right to act as a source of information are widely recognized as fundamental rights, critical not only to the development of the individual but also to the health and welfare of organizations and society in general.

Communication that liberates, enables people to articulate their own needs and helps them to act together to meet those needs. It enhances their sense of dignity and underlines their right to full participation in the life of their community. It aims to bring about structures in society, which is more just, more egalitarian, and more conducive to the fulfilment of rights, be they information or human rights.

Communication as discussed in the previous chapter is a large part of what a project does and should do. In the course of the day-to-day activities, a project manager is likely to receive tens of documents and attend numerous meetings where judgements are passed on future activities. Communication binds people together for a specific period of time, and during this time each person will operate under a legal and ethical framework.

As with most ethical issues, legality is considered to be a relevant issue, and in some instances, a measuring stick for what is considered to be ethical. Although ethics and legality are two separate issues, it is almost impossible to talk about one without the other. Organizations and their managers have few options when it comes to deciding what is legal and what is not. Codes of ethics are more frequently introduced to encompass the legality and social responsibilities of employees. Ethic codes and guidelines protect project managers and others from themselves, as well as from those who, they perceive, abuse the power of their position.

The Project Management Institute and the British Computer Society have typical codes that summarize the promises their professionals made to regulate themselves in the interest of society (see Appendix A).

6.3.1 Duties, responsibilities, and obligations

As discussed in the previous chapter, communication expresses itself in words and deeds and is also measured in the same way. All ethical actions must be able to challenge the principalities and powers. Communication that is undertaken in an ethical manner serves truth and challenges falsehood. Lies and half-truths are a great threat to communication. Communication should stimulate critical awareness of the reality and help a person to distinguish truth from falsehood and to disassociate that which is transient and trivial from that which is lasting and valuable. Often it is necessary to develop alternative forms of communication so that ethical words and deeds can be realized.

The translation of deeds comes from the acknowledgement that as a manager you have duties and responsibilities to promote and defend the right to communicate to your managers, staff, and other stakeholders in accordance with the following universal obligations:

- The obligation to respect the thoughts and ideas of all other people
- The obligation to respect the expression of thoughts and ideas by all other people
- The obligation to respect the privacy and security of all other people
- The obligation to respect the creative work of all other people
- The obligation to respect the pursuit of autonomous cultural development of other people
- The obligation to share our knowledge and experience with other people
- The obligation to participate in processes of public decision making and that capable leadership is chosen.

6.4 Governance

The modelling of ethical behaviour by organization leaders is positively related to Governance. Governance *refers to the processes and structure used to direct and manage an organization's operations and activities*. It defines the division of power, and establishes the mechanisms to achieve accountability between stakeholders, the, board of directors and management. Good governance systems help organizations focus on the activities that contribute most to their overall objectives: to utilize their resources effectively and ensure they are managed in the best interests of their principal stakeholders. At corporate level good governance is about:

- Respecting human rights and the rule of law
- Strengthening democracy
- Promoting transparency and capacity in private and public administration.

For those who work in project management, governance presents unprecedented challenges in political, economic, and societal systems. Two reports, one by Cadbury the other by Turnbull, highlighted a number of ethical and governance-related issues and recommended a number of changes. They include:

1. Cadbury (1992)
   - Separate audit and remuneration committees
   - Audit committee meet with auditors
   - Disclosure of remuneration of director's accounts
   - Three-year term of office
   - Nonexecutives have funds to take external advice

2. Turnbull (1999)
   - Accountability for disasters and crises
   - Risk to company must be disclosed
   - Directors must have effective system of internal controls
   - Consultation with board members
   - Provide the senior management and board with early warning mechanisms, and monitor the system of internal control.

It is clear that industry and commerce are not always benevolent, and regulation can be an effective way to serve societal objectives. The underlying implication in the corporate governance proposition is that we share enough common values that society can agree on good governance. In practice, however, only dramatic failures provide the basis for change, and this basis is known to be poor. For example, global scandals make headlines daily. Many of the recent incidents have one thing in common: they are a matter of ethics – or a lack thereof. To combat this, many global business are creating codes of conduct, like the ones companies such as IBM, Xerox, and Shell Oil have had for years. These three companies, and others, including Levi Strauss, Honeywell, Digital Equipment, Siemens, Nortel, ITT Corporation, Matsushita Electric, and Canon are taking their efforts further – by incorporating their messages into everyday business practices and making them living documents with global applicability.

Accommodating the principles outlined raises difficulties (that is, challenges) and opportunities for those who would offer governance issues in project management. So what is project governance and how can it be used to ensure the successful delivery of software projects?

6.4.1 Project governance

Within project management governance covers a number of functional disciplines, that include:

- Corporate strategy
- Operations (all services and products)
- Resource management
- Stakeholder relationships
- Professional standards
- Security and information
- Project boards.

Take, for example, the number of failed projects that have been reported in the computer press in the last 5 years. The focus within project management is increasingly moving towards developments in "good practice" that are orienting to an inclusive approach in it, a form of governance based on engagement with stakeholders. Specifically, the project management organizations should develop and manage their system of governance so that it facilitates:

- Stakeholders with a legitimate interest in the organizations activities and projects
- Stakeholder opinions must be valued and taken into account without compromising the organization's ability to make effective and just decisions
- Stakeholder engagement in helping to define and shape improvements in delivery and performance
- Stakeholder empowerment in delivering positive outcomes.

Project governance objectives should be incorporated into the formal "terms of reference" of the project manager. They should also form part of the project initiation document (PID). Including specific, measurable, achievable, relevant, and time-related (SMART) objectives into the appraisal system allows the organization to measure the governance benefits for those products or services you are contracted to provide. So what benefits can be expected from incorporating project governance into your systems of operation? Project governance helps:

- Reduce project risk
- Stimulate higher levels of stakeholder involvement
- Improve access to markets
- Enhance local performance

- Improve leadership
- Demonstrate transparency and accountability.

Within project governance, risk, transparency, and accountability lie not only with the sponsoring organization but also with "project boards" and such project boards are initiated to manage risk. Some boards by the nature of the mission of the organization require a certain number of people to come from a certain group or profession. Some project-related organizations will require a certain number of key business users on the board. For example, when undertaking rail transportation projects, membership of the board is likely to be made up with those involved in:

- Transport for London
- Network rail
- Strategic rail authority
- Train-operating companies
- Rail forums.

When this is the case, it is advisable to select candidates carefully with their risk quotient in mind. It is fine to have cautious or risk-taking people on the board, but it is equally important to have a balance. Only in this way can the board incorporate governance and produce balanced decisions time after time. Almost all strategic project decisions involve risk analysis, even if that analysis is taken for granted and dealt with/without ever mentioning risk analysis. A suggested integrated model for project governance is set out in Figure 6.1.

6.4.2 Managing stakeholder adjustments

The model defined in Figure 6.1 suggests that project governance places considerable accountability on stakeholders to make adjustments to their way of conducting business and doing things in synchronization with the providing organization. In making any such adjustments, stakeholders and their organizations will need to consider trade-offs in at least four areas:

1. Business (e.g. strategy and policy)
2. Financial (e.g. trading partners and markets)
3. Operations (e.g. business continuity and liability)
4. Compliance (e.g. business regulations and litigation).

Figure 6.1

Governance model.

Ethics	Leadership
Project Governance	
Risk	Stakeholders

Policies
Procedures
Standards
Codes of Conduct

Making adjustments to business practices and other processes must fit the circumstances of the organization. Project stakeholders may therefore decide that only some of the suggested practices are appropriate to their circumstances. This is not to suggest that the practices described previously should be adopted in their totality. It is simply a question of trade-off. It should also be noted that such trade-offs would be influenced by a number of factors; these factors are likely to be risk related and will include:

- An awareness of the organization's objectives and related significant risks
- The organization's policy on risk
- Whether the project and management strategies are effective and what needs to be done to put them into effect
- The fundamentals of good process and project management practices
- The scope of management and internal financial control
- The ways in which improvements can be made in order to mitigate risks
- The significant risks affecting the ability of the company to achieve its business objectives
- Propensity to change behaviours and working practices.

Two-way consultation can help identify if senior management has identified all the significant trade-offs and risks relevant to the objectives, particularly with regard to the changing internal and external environment. It also provides the project board with a sound foundation for its review of the effectiveness of internal control and for its "reporting and communication" to nonboard members on control (McManus, *Project Manager Today*, 2004).

6.5 Governance framework

Every organization must continually ask itself such questions as: "if we do such and such, what will our competition do?" Businesses often face difficult ethical problems and usually do not have time to reflect on all the consequences of a decision. Since the publication of *Cadbury and Turnbull*, greed and fraud have become the most prevailing and driving force found at the core of ethical dilemmas in corporate business today.

The pressure to make money (profits) leads many to cut corners, and take short cuts, or become focussed on getting their own share of the pie no matter what because everybody else is getting theirs. So often the utilitarian approach favoured by many managers gets knocked backed in this "greed is good culture" – working within a governance framework offers managers a way to reflect and focus on their individual responsibilities and accountabilities. A governance framework should aim to deliver assurances to stakeholders in relation to meeting an organization's objectives. Assurance on the system can be given with reference to independent assurance processes (internal and external) and achievement of satisfactory outcomes, or results.

The *Office of Government Commerce* offers some practical advice when putting together a governance framework. Consider:

- The nature of relationships with partners and providers
- The structure of the organization – for example, centralized
- The nature of the organization's business – such as policy work or operations
- The range of business functions undertaken and the commonalities between them
- The requirements for communication and data sharing across the business functions of the organization and its partners
- The distribution of authority and the extent of local autonomy
- The power and authority of central units
- The procedures and responsibilities for business planning and defining business strategy
- The geographic distribution of organizational units, business functions, and facilities such as information technology

- The existence of corporate-wide policies, such as for purchasing and procurement
- The role and authority of cross-divisional structures (for example, steering groups) in the organization and its partners
- The extent to which standards are enforced across the organization
- The extent to which work processes are common across the organization
- Requirements for security
- Internal control policies.

6.5.1 Managing governance objectives

A key element in securing the delivery of governance is the implementation of a sound system of internal control, encompassing an effective system of risk management that covers all risks. Internal control is the means by which an organization achieves its governance objectives. Leadership, risk, and stakeholder management is about managing the risks to achieve those objectives (Figure 6.2).

In project management, many distinct, yet sometimes interrelating processes will be found in the delivery of projects or supporting services, and these processes should be aligned to the governance framework. Such processes might include requirements planning, configuration management, change management, etc. Key processes will also include the development of

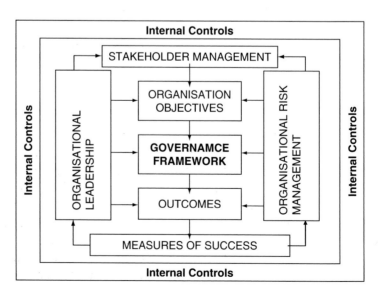

Figure 6.2
Integrated governance frameworks.

tactical plans and critical success factors (milestones) for delivery against objectives. They would also include communication of policy to stakeholders, and the establishment of procedures for the identification, management, and monitoring of risk. As discussed in Chapter 5, there should be an effective system of communication from and to the project board so that it is continuously aware of the progress on, and threats to, the delivery of the objectives. This should be supported by policies on "whistle blowing" (*that is, ethical resisters who publicly disclose unethical or illegal practices in the workplace*) to encourage openness, and adverse reporting that encourage reporting of adverse incidents on a nonpunitive basis in order that individuals and the organization can learn from experience and improve the quality of project delivery.

6.6 Governance problems and issues

As previously pointed out, senior management and the culture of an organization play a vital role in shaping the beliefs of what is right or wrong. What impairs governance is a belief by employees that it is there to protect senior management only from blame.

In the past 20 years, I have worked for several global organizations, many of which have operated quite comfortably outside a governance framework. As leaders and project managers we have a duty of caring the people who follow and work directly for us. This duty must extend to the pastoral and professional training of the individual – it must also extend to the instruction in ethics and governance. Most organizations claim a lot for enhancing their staff's professional development. On the contrary, research has found that in reality training and professionalism has been least important in priority of most organizations.

6.6.1 Governance audits and reporting

Cynics may see governance as window dressing. To avoid this apathy, governance should be subjected to frequent and independent and objective reviews. The results of these reviews should be communicated to the main or project board through the relevant committee appointed for this purpose (for example: Audit Committee, Governance Committee, and Risk Management Committee). Where controls are found to be inadequate, or are not complied with, there should be an action plan with dates set for corrective action and follow up (see Table 6.2).

Table 6.2 Example of follow-up audit questions

Governance follow-up questions	
Does the management give prompt and adequate attention to audit results, and take appropriate measures if problems are detected?	• Are internal audit results reported to the management promptly and accurately?
Yes	• Is information useful for improvement of operations regularly passed on to concerned departments such as the operations planning department?
No	• Does the internal audit section/department take the initiative in directing improvement measures such as the revision of internal rules in order to prevent the reoccurrence of problems?
Not sure	• Does the management appropriately monitor whether improvement measures directed to sections/departments are carried out?

The frequency and depth of these audit reviews will depend upon the degree of risk involved. It is also important that the reviews are conducted in a manner, and to a standard, that enables the board to derive meaningful assurance from them. Although a variety of review bodies may be involved, both internal and external, reflecting the differing technical expertise required, or statutory duties, there is a need to be aware of the danger of overlap or gaps in the review process. There is also the possibility of misunderstanding arising from differing approaches to the reviews.

Those responsible for conducting the governance audit should be informed of the need for their impartiality and independence from any aspects of management in the organization under audit. During the period covered by the audit, the auditor should not be employed by, serve as director for, or have any financial or close business relationship with, the entity, except as an independent professional adviser. The auditor should not have any close personal relationship with any senior participant in the management of the entity. It may be appropriate to remind the auditor of any existing statutory requirements relating to independence and to require the auditor to disclose any relationship likely to compromise their independence.

On completion of the audit, the board should ensure that the review is used to inform stakeholders and improve managers and that the organization learns from the report's recommendations.

6.7 Chapter summary – 10 key points

The most important points to take away from this chapter are:

1. The basis of ethical leadership is being an ethical person. Individuals must think of you as having certain traits, engaging in certain kinds of behaviours, and making decisions based upon ethical principles.
2. Project managers need to recognize the importance of proactively putting ethics at the forefront of their agenda; they need to make the ethical dimension of their leadership explicit and salient to their subordinates.
3. Understanding the organization and the extent and nature of the ethical problem is the leader's first step towards meeting this challenge.
4. Stakeholders have different legal, economic, and social relationship to a particular business project, sometimes a general stakeholder identification approach may not be too helpful in defining and explaining specific ethical obligations of managers to their stakeholders.
5. Overcoming apathy to ethical considerations is one task the project manager "must" take lead in. One of the key characteristics of ethical leadership is that of being a role model through visible action.
6. For leaders and project managers, ethics involves learning what is right and what is wrong, and then doing the right thing. Even so, the right thing is not nearly as basic as conveyed as it may depend on the situation.
7. Organizations and their managers have few options when it comes to deciding what is legal and what is not. Codes of ethics are more frequently introduced to encompass the legality and social responsibilities of employees.
8. The focus within project management is increasingly moving towards developments in "good practice", which are orienting to an inclusive approach in it a form of governance based on engagement with stakeholders.

9. The frequency and depth of audit reviews will depend upon the degree of risk involved. It is important that the reviews are conducted in a manner, and to a standard, that enables the board to derive meaningful assurance from them.

10. On completion of the audit, the board should ensure that the review is used to inform stakeholders and improve managers and that the organization learns from the report's recommendations.

6.8 Next chapter

In the next and final chapter, we will explore some selected case material, which supports and reinforces the messages outlined in the previous six chapters. The cases were selected for their ease of reading and on the basis of the information they provide.

Chapter references

Floyd, D. and J. McManus (2004) Stakeholder values: power and ethical perspective within project management, Economia Societae Istituzioni, 12(1).

Gert, B. (1998) Morality: Its Nature and Justification, Oxford University Press.

Hornum, F. and F. Stavish (1978) Criminology theory and ideology: four analytical perspectives in the study of crime and the criminal justice system. In Essays on the Theory and Practice of Criminal Justice, Rich, R. (ed.), Washington, DC, University Press, pp. 143–161.

McManus, J. (2004) Legitimacy and project governance. Project Manager Today, November/December, 35–39.

Rogerson, S. and D. Gotterbarn (1998) The ethics of software project management. In Ethics and Information Technology, Collste, G. (ed.), Delhi, India, New Academic Publishers, pp. 137–154.

Further reading

Fulton, J. (1998) Ethics and the 21st Century Manager, Masters Forum Publication.

Jones, R. (1986) Emile Durkheim: An Introduction to Four Major Works, Beverly Hills, CA, Sage Publications, Inc., pp. 60–81.

Mason, R. et al. (1995) Ethics of Information Management, Sage Publications.

7   Essays In Leadership

7.1 Essay No. 1: Personal leadership

This essay material is reproduced with permission from Paul Tarplett, Director, National and Local Services, OPM, November 2004, Copyright P. Tarplett, OPM.

7.1.1 Introduction

I have spent a lot of my working life over the last 20 years thinking about leadership and trying to help managers and others to provide better leadership for their people, their organizations, and most recently their partnerships and communities. I have kept testing my belief that good leadership does make a difference to performance and asking myself two related questions: what is it that distinguishes the better leaders from others? What can I do to help someone be a better leader? (It would be interesting to discuss your thoughts on my assumption and these questions.)

In reviewing recent writing on leadership, the most striking point is the sheer growth in volume of writing about it and the second is the confusion of ideas. There may be many reasons for this but I particularly liked Jim Collin's take that at the moment leadership has replaced God in filling a gap in our understanding. "Every time we attribute everything to 'leadership' we are no different from the people in the 1500s who attributed everything (they didn't understand such as famine and plague) to God" – Jim Collins, *Good to Great*.

This abundance of material reminded me of the importance of having an understanding of the schools of thought behind the various ideas; else, in the words of a colleague, we are simply in the hands of the airport lounge management gurus. So, in a separate paper, *Leadership, current thinking and how it developed* (also available on the OPM website), I have provided a summary of the development of thinking about leadership and some of the current fashionable views.

In this chapter, I would like to explain my thinking about leadership and how to develop it and, along the way, encourage you to think about your own views on these issues. To help you do so, there are questions (Sections 7.1.2–7.1.8) that you might like to use as the starting point for practical exercises, by yourself or with a group.

7.1.2 What do I think?

I think there are several important aspects to leadership, particularly for those who have senior roles in an organization. I think the argument about management vs leadership is pretty sterile. There are opportunities for people to show leadership, in most of the ways I would define it, at all levels in an organization and in nonorganisational settings. However, at senior levels, providing leadership is a core activity along with many other "managerial" functions.

7.1.2.1 Values

I think that leadership must above all else be rooted in ethics and the pursuit of a moral purpose. Leaders at whatever organizational level need to act with integrity based on sound ethical principles – *will Nolan do?* (see Appendix 1 for a reminder) *and if not what values or ethical standards guide your behaviour?* Because without this ethical base there is always the danger that all the skills of leadership can be used to dubious ends.

7.1.2.2 Professional or technical competence

Boyatzis described this as a "threshold" competence, i.e. it is the ticket to the game but not what distinguishes good leaders, which I think is fair enough, particularly since at the more senior levels, it is likely that you will be responsible for areas in which you have had little or no direct experience. Nevertheless I do think that it is worth stressing because competence gives you the potential credibility that you need with colleagues if they are to accept your leadership. However, this competence will relate to the context in which leadership is required. This can cause problems as people move from professional to senior managerial roles, when the basis of someone's competence – e.g. social work – may no longer be adequate in a situation that requires different skills.

I do not expect the people whom I am willing to follow to be "brilliant", but I do expect anyone I am following to know enough to be able to understand what others are saying and take good ideas when they are offered. Ignorance of context or underlying stupidity probably disqualifies someone from leadership. However, I will not follow those that are brilliant if they lack integrity or even decent humanity. *What's your bottom line on this – does competence matter and if so what sort?*

7.1.2.3 Sense making and mental models

This builds on the previous point: I cannot see how you can lead without having some model of how the world, your organization, and people work. It is such models that, in times of turbulent changes, enable you to make enough sense of the world so as not to be paralysed. (In his book, *Images of Organization*, Gareth Morgan identifies some of the dominant mental models about organizational life). This sense making, which may be tentative and up for debate, allows the collective to act and this seems a prerequisite for leadership. If this model(s) is not explicit then you cannot hold it up to the light and check its accuracy. This reflecting on one's mental models is called "double loop" learning because as well as looking at problems and their ostensible causes one is also looking at the tools, which one uses to analyse these problems and checking their suitability.

7.1.3 So what are the models or mind sets that you find most useful as a leader?

7.1.3.1 Learning and building distributed leadership

Peter Senge's idea that the role of the leader is building a learning organization that follows from the above, since he sees a key part of this task as helping people to unmask their mental models. Again it seems to me that leadership requires a willingness to learn and in organizational terms to help others learn. Without this, you end up with the heroic leader model, which even if it works in the short term has the longer term effect of disempowering others and creating the classic group of "powerless" staff blaming "them" and being unwilling to take responsibility for solving problems. A more appropriate mind set is to recognize that leadership needs to be fluid, to move even within a particular meeting to match abilities and needs. Consequently, the deal I want with staff is for them to use their intelligence and good judgement and in return to give them the space and support to do so. I hope that in this context, we will give each other the benefit of the doubt if something goes wrong and seek to learn from it rather than to lay blame.

7.1.3.2 Some supporting quotes

"Organisations transform when they can establish mechanisms for learning in the dailiness of organisational life . . . Leaders in a culture of change create these conditions for daily learning and they learn to lead by experiencing such learning at the hands of other leaders."

"It's a question of building strong institutions not creating heroic leaders (quoting Mintzberg)"

"The chief role of leadership is to mobilise the collective capacity to challenge difficult circumstances." – Michael Fullan

Again, what is your take on this – how important is it to build opportunities for learning and what have you done, what do you need to do?

7.1.4 Do those who work for you show the leadership you want?

7.1.4.1 Social process and leadership style

The entire above have strands of interaction with people within them but since leadership does not exist without "followers", it is fundamentally about relationships. The question then is what can leaders do to build effective relationships with others? I think the Goleman Emotional Intelligence (EI) stuff is helpful here because of the connections it makes, first between self-awareness and self-control – without which you lose the ability to choose what behaviours to offer in a particular situation. And second between the behaviours that you choose and their long-term impact on relationships and performance.

A writer called Zaleznic observed of this approach that "leadership is a psychodrama in which a brilliant lonely person must gain control of himself/herself as a precondition for controlling others." I think this is a bit harsh! Yes we can find examples of brilliant but dysfunctional people providing effective leadership in certain situations but these do not seem to offer much insight into what the rest of us might usefully do in our own situations. Yes, it is also probably true that self-control on its own is not enough but who said it was! And self-control does give you choice over the behaviour that you use and some behaviours seem to be a lot more productive over the long term. (These were summarized in the paper on the development of leadership thinking.) Since these behaviours fit with my own experiences and prejudices, I find it relatively easy to agree with this argument.

Michael Fullan also makes a case for the primacy of relationships in performance improvement, to paraphrase "when relationships improved results got better and when they got worse results got worse." This may be right but I think it would be a mistake to see this as just a question of style, I think it also reflects some of the other aspects of leadership identified above such as sense making and competence.

7.1.5 So, how important are the various elements of EI in your thinking about leadership?

7.1.5.1 What, no vision?

I am a bit ambivalent about vision, despite Goleman's findings and the whole of the transformational leadership models. On the one hand, I agree that people need to feel that they are being offered more than hanging on by their finger tips until they fall or die but on the other hand, many visions – particularly corporate ones – can seem so far removed from every day life and indeed from the interests of most staff that they may even make matters worse by making people more cynical. The following quote captured my own worries quite well "In this new organisation (Apple) employees were supposed to work hard, ceaselessly, uncomplainingly and even for relative low pay not just to produce and sell a product but to realise the vision of the messianic leader." – Khurana (2002).

I suppose there are two issues for me – one is whose vision is it and the second is – in whose benefit is it being pursued. As a follower, I would want to have a chance to influence the vision and I would want the vision to contribute to something I believe in. Both these conditions can be met (more easily in the public sector?) but I am not sure they always are. So let us come back to moral purpose and ask what are we in this for and what does that mean for what we are trying to achieve over the next year or so and let us build a shared vision of what this might look like with staff and other key stakeholders.

7.1.6 Is the vision you have for your organization or your part of it shared by enough people? Does it help to motivate you and your people?

7.1.6.1 Influence–power–politics

Power and politics are often neglected in books on leadership. Exceptions to this are a recent article about Bill Bratton who has turned round several failing public sector organizations in the USA such as NYPD. He has a four-stage "tipping point" leadership model which includes getting managers to think about problems in different ways, focussing resources on where they will make most impact, challenge to raise motivation, and *politically dealing with opponents*. In *Creating Public Value*, Mark Moore comments on the related theme of legitimacy, arguing that it is this that gives you the power to act in the public sector and survive even if things go wrong.

The management of power and politics is a central part of what effective leaders do well. This is because leaders can do a little on their own but generally they need to win others support in order to make a difference. Sometimes this can be commanded through line authority but even here, there is a considerable amount of extra discretionary effort to be accessed. And many leadership situations sit outside the framework of line authority. So we need to influence others in order to make leadership effective, sometimes as we have already seen we can draw upon "expert" power and sometimes on line authority and sometimes neither. We can then fall back on our social skills and our ability to build a common attractive vision.

However, leaders also need to be able to read the politics of a situation in order to make good judgements about when to act, when to do nothing, how to speak, whom to speak privately, etc. (If you have ever seen Shakespeare's *Julius Caesar*, you might recall how well Cassius does this.) However, reading a situation well is not enough; you also need to be able to assemble the necessary power to make something happen. You might like to think about the possible sources of such power and how you can access them. In *Working the Shadow Side*, Gerard Egan identifies the following potential sources of power:

- Your authority, what you control, particularly control over resources
- Your competencies or recognized expertise
- Influencing styles and skills

- Your personal qualities and their attractiveness to others
- Relationships and networks.

He suggests the following possible strategies for building power:

- Understanding organizational needs and presenting your goals in a way which shows how they contribute to the bigger picture.
- Building common goals so that others see their agendas in terms of what you want to achieve.
- Watch and learn what works inside your organization. For example, analyse people's motivation, is it self-interest (individual or group); institutional enhancement or mixed? Watch activities to do with acquiring scarce resources such as capital, budgets, desired positions, policy, and key decisions. These insights will reveal what is really going on, which may not be what people say.
- Identify key players and their interests and address them, i.e. find out what people want and see if you can give it to them.
- Use alliances and coalitions to strengthen your position – it is harder to achieve anything if you are isolated.
- Make and withdraw deposits into "relationship bank accounts", e.g. making concessions or supporting others gives you something to draw upon later – reciprocity is understood (e.g. if you are going to lose a decision, try to do so with grace so that people feel that they owe you).

Recognizing the realities of power and managing the associated politics is often seen as a negative behaviour but for me, that depends on how it is done and the rationale behind it.

7.1.7 Think about your own experience, perhaps some critical and contested decisions that were made – who won and who lost, or did you find a way not to make it seem win/lose?

7.1.7.1 Good judgement

Virtually all the above imply the need to make judgements particularly at the point in which thought becomes action or not. Judgement is so integral; it almost goes without saying, yet I have decided to make it explicit because it is the focal point of leadership.

145

7.1.7.2 Some supporting quotes

"What would happen if we started from the premise that we can't measure what matters and go from there? Then instead of measurement we'd have to use something very scary: it's called judgement. A society without judgement is a society that's lost. And that's what bureaucracy does: it drives out judgement' – the Observer, 26 January 2003, *The scary world of Mr Mintzberg.*

Lets get to this: "We're glad to have you with our organisation. Our number one aim is to provide outstanding public value to local citizens. Set both your personal and professional goals high."

Rule No 1: use your good judgement in all situations. Rule No 2: there are no more rules! – Barry Quirke, C.E. LB of Lewisham.

7.1.7.3 Action and achievement

"When all is said and done, more is said than done." This is certainly true of leadership! Ultimately, leadership should be judged by what you do and what it achieves. Both outcome and process are important. The ends do not always justify the means but on the other hand if nothing is achieved then some soul searching is probably required. Again a quote that illustrates this:

"Moral purpose cannot be just stated, it must be accompanied by strategies for realising it and those strategies are the leadership actions that energise people to pursue a desired goal." – Michael Fullan.

Jim Collins has argued that there are a few key areas where effective leaders apply their judgement and act. I do not wish to rehearse them all because there is not space and that is his argument not mine but I do like the notion of getting the right people into the organization and the wrong ones out because it strikes me as an essential task for a senior organizational leader. The others I liked were:

- Be willing to face brutal facts but be optimistic about your ability to succeed
- Build a culture of discipline so that you do not need lots of rules
- Be willing to challenge "good enough" to make something excellent
- Be persistent – stay with a chosen strategy – do not keep bringing in new initiatives.

7.1.8 What leadership achievement are you most proud of?

7.1.8.1 Is leadership transferable?

Leadership is practised differently by everyone and rightly so because each of us has to find our own way of doing it if it is to be authentic. It is also contextual. However, there are common strands and someone who learned to be an effective leader in one situation could take useful skills and learning with them to another situation but they would have to be open to learning about the new context and the new people they are working with – is my view – *what do you think?*

Jim Collins in *Good to Great* comments that 10 out of 11 great CEOs came from within the company, their competitors who did less well turned to outsiders.

7.1.9 Summary

I had not written this with the OPM model of leadership in mind (Figure 7.1 gives the existing OPM model) but if I look at it, now I can see that it is not a bad fit with what I believe about leadership, i.e. it should serve a deserving purpose and should be based on sound values, expressed through ethical behaviour. Effective leaders will also have a good understanding of the context, a set of interpersonal and political skills and a willingness to use them to make good judgements and act to achieve results. They will learn from their successes and failures, they will encourage others to learn and provide the space and encouragement for distributed leadership to develop. (An amended version of the model designed to reflect the points that I have here is given in Figure 7.2.)

7.1.9.1 How can you develop leaders?

If you agree with the earlier point that leadership is a social phenomenon, then it opens up several possibilities for development:

- 360-degree feedback will probably be helpful given that most of us have imperfect self-awareness.
- It will probably be more effective to teach leadership and followership together, particularly if you buy my argument that a key leadership role is developing distributed leadership and building a culture in which leadership can move between people according to need. This suggests that leadership is best explored in work groups. Working in groups

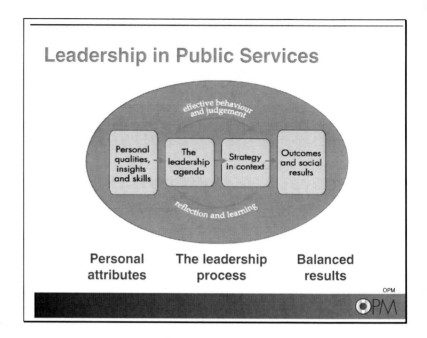

Figure 7.1
OPM leadership model.

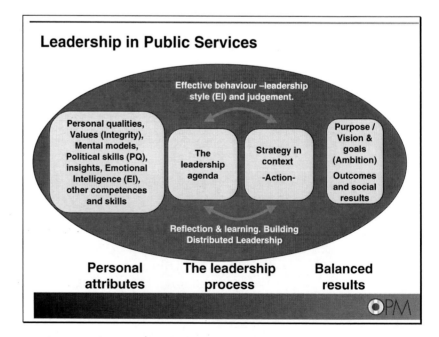

Figure 7.2
Amended version of
leadership model.

of people who interact with each other would also enable an exploration of role expectations and negotiation of a specific psychological contract.

Competencies may be a useful method for capturing the leadership expectations that we have of people in different roles. Competencies would also help to identify what it is that people in these roles need to learn to do. If the 360-degree feedback is based on these competencies then the feedback gives a good indication of the extent to which the recipients of it are currently meeting these behavioural expectations.

Leaders will benefit from having the space to reflect on their own views about leadership and their answers to the following questions. *How would you answer these questions?*

- Leadership is individual but there are common challenges
- Being clear about your value base – what do you stand for?
- What is your style and does it reflect your stated values?
- Do you have the competence required by the situation(s) in which you are providing leadership?
- What is your mental model(s)?
- Do you provide opportunities for learning – yours and others?
- Are you reading the politics of situations well and acting accordingly?
- Are you reviewing your judgements and learning from them?
- What are you trying to achieve and how are you doing?

7.1.9.2 What does this mean to you?

If I go back to my opening questions I think I have given my answer to the first one (what makes for an effective leader?) and suggested some ways in which the second (how can I help people to become better leaders) might be answered but I would really encourage you to have your views on this.

I would like to encourage you to argue with my views and come to your own conclusions because good outcomes for me would be for you:

- To have tested your own thinking about leadership
- To have a clear view of the leadership your team, organization and related partnerships need and how to develop it
- To be clear about any changes that you want to make to improve your effectiveness as a leader.

In doing this, you might find it helpful to answer some of the challenge questions I have posed or you may want to suggest different ones and offer answers to those.

Despite some differences in organizational detail, there is generally considerable agreement about what a core set of leadership competencies may be. However, experience strongly suggests that the balance and application of these competencies have to align with the organizational and environmental contexts within which the leader operates. These contexts are in continuous flux and as a result the application of qualities, knowledge, and skills needed from leaders changes over time. And, because change itself requires leadership, an important leadership attribute is the ability to constantly assess and develop the balance and application of the competencies which are required from oneself as a leader. Hence, our model is a contingent one, placing emphasis on the need to develop and deploy effective judgement and constantly to reflect and learn. In our survey responses, we find that many people in senior positions recognize the imperative of these leadership development needs, placing them at the top of their personal development agenda.

In Figure 7.2, it is the leadership process which connects the personal attributes of the individual to the range of balanced results which must be achieved by the organization. Central to the leadership process is the individual's ability to formulate a leadership agenda that fits the organizational and environmental contexts, and then to express that as strategy or direction for the organization. Helen Brown, Robin Douglas, *Leadership in Public Services* (OPM, 2000).

References

Alvesson and Deetz (2000) Doing Critical Management Research. London, Sage.

Beverly Alimo Metcalf and John Alban Metcalf (2004) Leadership in public sector organisations. In: Leadership in Organisations. John Storey (ed.).

Brown, R. and R. Douglas (2000) Leadership in Public Services. London, OPM. OPM is an independent, not-for-profit, *public interest company*, working with people to develop high quality management, professional practice and public engagement in organisations that aim to improve social results. OPM is based in London England.

Chan Kim and Renee Mauborgne (2004) Tipping point leadership (about Bill Bratton). In: View. NHS Modernisation Agency.

Richard Boyatzis (1982) The Competent Manager. New York, Wiley–Interscience.

Jim Collins (2001) Good to Great. Random House.

Gerard Egan (1994) Working the Shadow Side. Jossey Bass.

Michael Fullan (2001) Leading in a Culture of Change. San Francisco, Jossey Bass.

Daniel Goleman (1998) Working with Emotional Intelligence. Bloomsbury.

Daniel Goleman, Richard Boyatzis, and Annie McKee. The New Leaders.

Khurana (2002) The curse of the superstar CEO. Harvard Business Review, 3–8 September 2002.

Mark Moore (1995) Creating Public Value. Harvard.

Gareth Morgan (1997) Images of Organization (2nd edition). London, Sage.

Peter Senge (1990) The Fifth Discipline. Doubleday.

John Storey (ed.) (2004) Leadership in Organisations. Routledge.

Zaleznic (1992) Managers and leaders are they different? Harvard Business Review, March–April 1992.

Appendix 1: Nolan standards

Selflessness

Holders of public office should take decisions solely in terms of the public interest. They should not do so in order to gain financial or other material benefits for themselves, their family, or their friends.

Integrity

Holders of public office should not place themselves under any financial or other obligation to outside individuals' organizations that might influence them in the performance of their official duties.

Objectivity

In carrying out public business, including making public appointments, awarding contracts, or recommending individuals for rewards and benefits, holders of public office should make choices on merit.

Accountability

Holders of public office are accountable for their decisions and actions to the public and must submit themselves to whatever scrutiny is appropriate to their office.

Openness

Holders of public office should be as open as possible about all the decisions and actions that they take. They should give reasons for their decisions and restrict information only when the wider public interest clearly demands.

Honesty

Holders of public office have a duty to declare any private interests relating to their public duties and to take steps to resolve any conflicts arising in a way that protects the public interest.

Leadership

Holders of public office should promote and support these principles by leadership and example.

7.2 Essay No. 2: Leading virtual teams

This essay material is reproduced with permission from Dr David Gould, University of Phoenix; this article was originally published in the Boeing Manager Magazine in May 1997.

7.2.1 Introduction

Teamwork has been around since before our ancestors gathered up their spears and learned how to work together to gang up on mastodons and saber-toothed tigers. Many experts agree that teams are the primary unit of performance in any organization. Today, there is a new kind of team – a "virtual" team made up of people who communicate electronically. Its members may hardly ever see each other in person. In fact, they may never meet at all, except in cyberspace.

7.2.2 Work from home

To some people, working alone at home is a terrific option. They like the idea of sitting at their terminals in robe and slippers, the cat curled at their feet. Others find the idea a little lonely and somehow disconcerting. They worry that they would pine for the chatty atmosphere around the water cooler. However you feel about virtual teams, there are more and more of them, and they offer some definite benefits.

For one thing, there is no need for office or parking space. For another, more people can be included in the labour pool. Air pollution and congestion are reduced when people do not commute. Virtual teaming offers more flexibility for workers and organizations alike.

Software designed just for virtual teams, called "groupware", is growing increasingly sophisticated. (Lotus Notes and Exchange are two popular programs.) Videoconference programs are also available, but so far they are unwieldy and expensive, requiring too much bandwidth to be practical. The work of virtual teams can also be enhanced by the use of a Web site. It is a handy place to store and distribute graphic materials, schedules, flowcharts, reference materials, and more.

7.2.3 Research data

Virtual teaming is not something anyone planned. It happened because the technology was there. But how well are these teams really working and what can be done to make them more effective? What are some of the benefits of the virtual team? What are the pitfalls? Do unsupervised employees take advantage of the situation? What leadership skills are needed to make the virtual team work well?

For the answers to these questions, I did a research study based on in-depth interviews and one case study. I studied people in virtual teams of up to 100 people. They were doing all kinds of work: planning a conference, editing a text book, developing software, even starting a company. Most of the virtual teams relied on telephones and e-mail. A few of them used telephone conferencing. Most of the teams were brought together for one project, then disbanded. Most of the team members worked on the team's tasks full time, but some were volunteers working after hours. A lot of teams would never have been formed without today's technology. The expense and logistical problems would have been insurmountable.

7.2.4 Characteristics of virtual teams

Here is what the data reveal about the virtual team phenomenon:

Virtual teams get the job done. Most of the teams I studied achieved the goals set for them. In only one instance did a team fail to attain its goals, and this failure could not be connected to the fact that the team was a virtual team.

People can be trusted. The question many managers ask is, "Can you trust people you can't see to do their work?" For the teams in my study, the answer was clearly yes. Tasks would not have been accomplished if the work had not been done. While participants acknowledged that this was a potential problem ("Your manager doesn't see you. Out of sight, out of mind," one of them said), it did not seem to have been an actual problem.

Few virtual teams are 100 percent virtual. Virtual teams tend to have some face-to-face meetings. In the study, face-to-face contact was fairly unimportant in teams with relatively independent team members engaged in individual work projects. However, it was important in teams with interdependent members. As one team member commented, "Face-to-face is very important. You yell at the woman [from the phone company] when your phone bill is messed up, not because she is responsible but because you don't know her face. Once you've met, you have more compassion and understanding for your fellow team members."

Virtual teams take on the same basic structure as "real" teams. The teams I studied showed the same dynamics that researchers have discovered in "real" teams. The early stages are characterized by a certain amount of randomness, chaos, and ad hoc decision making. As the team matures, processes are put into place and the team becomes more efficient.

7.2.5 Leading virtual teams

I was particularly interested in learning about effective leadership techniques for virtual teams. Virtual team leaders are operating within a different framework. Some of the behaviours considered that good management practices were changed, or even eliminated, because the team was physically separated.

Individual recognition, for instance, was infrequent and when it occurred, it was via e-mail or a telephone call. An e-mail message like this was typical "Now that the conference has come and gone, I just wanted to send a note of thanks to all of you who submitted ... I appreciated all of your hard work in creating materials and getting them to me on time throughout the process." Some people felt online recognition was helpful; others were uncomfortable with it. They felt somehow communication should be done in person. One team leader arranged a voice conference call to make her praise public and to ensure that everyone heard it at once.

Celebrations of team accomplishments pretty much went by the board in the teams I studied. The team leaders rarely if ever initiated celebrations. Comments from team members ranged from the barely festive, "Should we find ourselves in the same town at the same time, we would meet and celebrate past performance," to the rather plaintive, "There were no celebrations of any sort – sounds drab, doesn't it?" Some teams met to celebrate in person at the completion of the project, but for many, geography and expense made this impossible. So far, no one seems to have discovered a technique for successful virtual partying.

Team leaders did, however, occasionally offer support and coaching to team members. One team leader, who provided verbal support in the editing of a textbook by a far-flung group of scholars around the world, put it this way "Challenge, encouragement, and coaching are at the very nature of the editing and authoring process."

7.2.6 Dealing with communication problems

While most virtual team members had a positive experience overall, the biggest area of complaint involved communication problems. These complaints fell into several categories. The first was lack of project visibility. Team members knew what they were doing on an individual basis, but they were not always sure where their pieces fit into the whole puzzle. Second, there were sometimes problems in actually getting hold of people. One team member said: "(It's frustrating) not being able to get a response from people as soon as you like. Weeks can slip by and we are all doing other jobs. You send out a question and in some cases an answer never comes back. You don't know how to interpret it. They don't want to answer or what?" Occasionally, there were constraints from the technology. "Communication in a virtual environment has its own set of challenges," said one team member. "It's sometimes difficult to derive the meaning from text-based messages, especially if the person is attempting to be sarcastic or facetious. Guidelines on how to let others know the intention of your message, whether it's through the use of emoticons or what not, are important."

For the uninitiated, "emoticons" are those expressive little faces made out of parentheses, pound keys, percent signs, and so forth. Human ingenuity seems to have triumphed once again, finding a way to add nuance and feeling to electronic text.

7.2.7 Tips on alleviating communication problems

Include face-to-face time if at all possible
Have an initial meeting for the team members to get together, meet each other, and socialize. Meet face-to-face periodically throughout the life of the project. These meetings will help to establish ties and relationships among team members. It is especially important in creating an effective working environment where the team members are interdependent.

Give team members a sense of how the overall project is going
Send team members copies of the updated project schedule or provide an electronic view of the project schedule on line using

the Internet. Project management schedule charts can be published on the Internet using the team's Web site. The primary idea here is to improve the quality and type of communications with all team members. They need to know where they fit in the big picture.

Establish a code of conduct to avoid delays

The code could include a principle of acknowledging a request for information within 24 or 48 h. A complete response to a request might require more time, but at least the person requesting the information would know that the request will be addressed. No one likes to feel that his or her request has dropped off the edge of the earth.

Do not let team members vanish

Use the Internet or workgroup calendaring software to store team members' calendars. While this could be difficult to maintain on a daily basis, it should not be difficult to keep up with scheduled out-of-town absences such as vacations or business travel. Another approach is to agree that team members will let everyone know when they will be going out of town. Electronic mail with a distribution list is both an effective and efficient way to avoid MIAs.

Augment text-only communication

The Internet is a good place to store charts, pictures, or diagrams so everyone can have a look. The fax machine, once a modern marvel but now surprisingly oldfashioned, can help here too.

Develop trust

Charles Handy, an author and management consultant, addresses this issue quite clearly. "If we are to enjoy the efficiencies and other benefits of the virtual organization, we will have to rediscover how to run organizations based more on trust than on control. Virtuality requires trust to make it work: Technology on its own is not enough."

7.2.8 Trust

The issue of trust is at the centre of successful virtual team management. The fact is that old-style command and control management, based on constant scrutiny, is simply impossible in a virtual environment. "Whips and chains are no longer an alternative," says Warren Bennis, professor of business at the University of Southern California. "Leaders must learn how to change the nature of power and how it's employed. If they don't, technology will. Virtual leadership is about keeping everyone focused as old structures, including old hierarchies, crumble." It is an idea echoed by Raymond Smith, CEO of Atlantic Bell, a company obviously interested in the future of electronic communication "Leadership on (virtual) teams will likely be determined by who's most expert on the matter at hand – not by corporate hierarchy."

Further reading

For more information on virtual teams, read Going Virtual by Ray Grenier and George Metes, published by Prentice-Hall; and Charles Handy's article "Trust and the Virtual Organization" *Harvard Business Review* (May–June 1995).

7.3 Essay No. 3: Evolutionary leadership

This essay material is reproduced with permission from Pegasus Communication. This article was originally published in *The Systems Thinker®* Newsletter (Vol. 12, No. 9), copyright 2001 by Stefan C. Gueldenberg and Werner Hoffmann.

7.3.1 Introduction

Why do some companies grow while others shrink? Why are some firms extraordinarily successful over the years while others – even those in the same industry – slide from crisis to crisis? Why do so many brilliant management strategies lead firms directly into decline or not produce the anticipated results? And why do so many classical theories of business administration fail to explain these phenomena and help company leaders avoid or overcome these problems? Executives today are constantly seeking to predict how their organizations and the marketplace will behave. But because many leaders continue to use traditional reductionist methods to understand organizational behaviour – ones that focus more on *symptoms* than on *causes* of a company's success – they fail to gain real insight into how to build and sustain that success. The result is often reactive, crisis-driven management with unanticipated side effects and unforeseen outcomes. Contrary to this rigid perception of organizations as predictable machines, some management thinkers have come to view them as complex and evolving organisms. Accordingly, the tendency in the business world to define companies in terms of simple formulas and numerical results is slowly being replaced by the recognition that, to be effective in leading organizations, we must think of them in terms of the underlying structures and dynamic patterns of behaviour that produce those results. In other words, we must begin to complement or replace linear thinking about how our business work with nonlinear approaches by applying the principles and tools of system dynamics.

7.3.2 System dynamics theory

In his classic 1961 book, *Industrial Dynamics*, Massachusetts Institute of Technology, Prof. Jay Forrester originated the ideas and methodology of system dynamics. He pointed out that the traditional approaches of the management sciences could not satisfactorily explain the causes of corporate growth or decline because they focussed on simply explaining *behaviour*. He believed that a system's behaviour is actually a product of its *structure* and that leaders should seek to identify where changes in structure might lead to significant, enduring improvements. They could then design organizational policies and processes that would lead to even greater success. In order for managers to undertake this design process, Forrester advocated that they must analyse their organizations using dynamic models. For this purpose, he developed tools such as causal loop and stock and flow diagrams. These tools serve to illustrate the interconnected feedback loops that form a complex system. By identifying these feedback loops, management can figure out a system's basic patterns of behaviour, which include growth (caused by positive feedback), balance (caused by negative feedback), oscillations (caused by negative feedback combined with a time delay), and further complex interconnections. Applied to organizations, this way of thinking challenges the notion of measuring success only through financial results. Because people can see financial results, they think they have control over them. But these results are actually produced by the organization's underlying structures. These structures consist of:

- *Organizational architecture:* the basic organizational design (such as the functions or divisions that the company includes) and the governance system (such as the planning and control system)
- *Organizational routines:* standard operating procedures, decision-making processes, behavioural archetypes
- *Tangible and intangible resources:* financial capital, human resources, buildings, machinery, land, brands
- *Organizational knowledge and value base:* patents, core competencies, cultural beliefs, attitudes.

When we focus on systemic structures and behavioural patterns, we gain the knowledge to design our organizations to produce desirable day-to-day results in areas such as profits, employee motivation, customer satisfaction, and so on (see "Structure, Behaviour, and Results"). The basic idea of the dynamic approach is that, although people shape their organizations, their behaviour is ultimately influenced, and therefore limited, by the organizational framework in which they operate. Consequently, leadership means much more than optimizing business for short-term outcomes; it involves creating and cultivating structures and enabling organizational behaviours that guarantee the viability of the whole firm. Therefore, in order to manage their organizations successfully, leaders must realize that the best way to achieve sustainable results is not by relying only on what they *see* or *measure* but by:

- Describing and assessing the observable behaviour of the system
- Understanding the interdependencies between a system's behaviour and its underlying structure
- Making assumptions about and modelling these interdependencies using system dynamics tools
- Finding and implementing policies to redesign the structure of the system in order to improve its performance.

Building on this system dynamics foundation, we propose to take leadership one step further, to what we call *evolutionary leadership*. The natural process of evolution offers a compelling model of how leaders might intentionally design and guide growth and balancing processes to create a viable organization. Evolutionary leadership involves the deliberate interplay of two management functions: *strategic management* (designing structures and processes that *stimulate* growth) and *management control* (guiding the external and internal factors that *regulate* growth). But before we explore the synergy between these two functions, we need to talk about how evolution works in nature and in organizations.

7.3.3 Evolutionary theory in organizations

Evolutionary theory has been the predominant paradigm in natural sciences for more than a century. Recently, theorists and practitioners in the social and management sciences have begun to adopt the ideas of evolutionary theory as a framework for describing and analyzing organizational development. The basic concept these pioneers have set forth is that processes of variation, selection, and retention as well as the struggle for scarce resources trigger the evolution of an organization. Sociocultural evolution differs from biological evolution in that it allows for the intentional variation and selection of ideas. In this context, an organization's fitness – its "viability" or ability to survive and thrive – depends on how its decisions and strategies affect its position in product and resource markets and on its legitimacy from the point of view of important stakeholders. Chilean neurobiologists Humberto Maturana and Francisco Varela have deeply influenced thinking about viability with their theory that living systems are complex systems that can self-generate. A system dies when it loses its ability to renew itself. In the business world, a company that fails to renew itself by changing its strategic orientation and/or internal structure in response to shifting conditions will die. In contrast, a viable organization is one that can continually create its own future and thereby assure its fitness in an evolutionary sense. But how does a viable organism develop this capacity to self-generate? According to Maturana and Varela, it happens when the organism:

- Preserves its identify by repeatedly drawing system boundaries (i.e. defining what is "internal" and "external")
- Maintains its ability to adapt to a changing environment.

Within ever-changing environments, external forces constantly threaten the existence of a species by altering its living space. To survive, a species must adapt to the changing conditions successfully without losing its identity. For example, in nature, many kinds of birds have adapted from natural to urban environments, but not all have managed to do so. In the banking industry, banks have profoundly shifted their strategies in the past decade in response to technology changes and new competitors. Many brick-and-mortar institutions have gone "virtual". In doing so, they are able to maintain their existence by simultaneously preserving their identity while adapting their strategy and structure to a changing environment.

The key to an organization's survival lies in mastering the trade-off between preserving its identity and adapting to a changing environment. Leaders do so through strategic thinking and acting, and by asking how they can maintain the fit of the organizational structure and its environment. There are two ways to achieve this goal:

- Maintain your identity and structure and avoid fundamental adaptations by changing the environment or searching for an appropriate new environment

- Fundamentally change your structure and redefine your identity to re-establish a fit between the organization and its ever-changing environment.

In reality, most organizations choose adaptation strategies that lie somewhere between these two extremes. Organizations can only make alterations to the extent that their structures and resources make modifications possible. A firm has a good chance to success-fully adapt to a changing environment when it has a strong learn-ing capacity, that is, the ability to anticipate, influence, and quickly react to environmental changes, along with the ability to recognize, vary, and advance the underlying mechanisms of the learning process itself. For example, Shell Oil enhances its learning capacity by combining strategic planning and organizational learning through *scenario planning*. Scenario planning provides a mechanism for thinking in alternatives and making underlying assumptions explicit. This process reduces the company's risk of encountering negative surprises and increases the speed with which it can imple-ment changes. In short, organizational learning is dynamic feed-back processes that can help organizations remain viable and therefore survive the external pressures of natural selection (see "The Evolutionary Cycle in Organizations").

7.3.4 Growth and balance

In addition to having the ability to adapt and learn, systems must be able to grow. Generally speaking, growing means incor-porating more and more available resources – like nutrients for a plant or natural or human resources for a company – in order to become larger and larger. For a company, growth can mean an increase in market share or market value. But is growth in itself sufficient for survival? Clearly, the answer is no, because nothing grows forever. But where and what are the *limits to growth?* In nature, reinforcing processes, such as population growth, are slowed by balancing processes, such as limited food supplies and the spread of diseases. If normal balancing processes are not blocked and assert themselves before a population reaches the limits of its habitat, that species can maintain a harmonious rela-tionship with its environment. Such balancing processes ensure that the evolving system remains within a viable range of activi-ties, in this case, healthy population density. Indeed, these bal-ancing processes are more crucial than reinforcing processes, in that they keep the overall system alive. If, on the other hand, important balancing processes are missing, the species might become extinct by overtaxing the resources in its environment. Are there similar natural boundaries to the development of social systems? The answer is yes. For example, a firm's development can be limited by its production capacity, the size of its market, or the number of its competitors. The faster the company grows, the more rapidly it reaches these boundaries. From time to time, such limits to growth can change. For example, shifts in market conditions, such as those created by the Internet boom or the world oil crisis of the 1970s, can increase or decrease the time it takes an organization to reach a certain limit, unless people find ways to use their limited resources more efficiently.

We can say that an organization is evolving when its configuration, routines, tangible and intangible resources, knowledge, and value base develop in accordance with the changing external environment. Scientists now know that most healthy living systems follow a developmental path described as *punctuated equilibrium* – periods of balanced growth that are interrupted by periods of exponential growth. We regularly underestimate the tremendous power of exponential or reinforcing growth. We tend to assume that growth is linear and increases consistently over time. However, exponential growth happens much more precipitously. If we observe the two over a short period of time, exponential growth approximates linear growth. Over a longer period, however, the gap between the two becomes enormous. Because human beings tend to perceive short-term rather than long-term changes, we often reach the boundaries of exponential growth faster than we anticipated, often completely unexpectedly. We see this happen to companies when booming success is followed by equally dramatic failure. For example, cellular telephone companies experienced this phenomenon when they projected that their sales would continue to increase at a high level. But they eventually saturated the market and experienced declining sales. For this reason, unless we understand and anticipate the impact and boundaries of exponential growth, we will have a distorted perception of the evolutionary process, leading to unpleasant surprises and even to an existential crisis for the whole enterprise. Organizations sustain themselves when they attain a balanced evolution – offsetting reinforcing growth action with timely balancing impulses. Sustaining this balance is the only way to ensure that companies remain in the realm of "sound growth" as they develop and that they do not exceed the limits of their environment or resources. Balanced evolution plays an especially critical role during periods of exponential growth, when the organization is at a much higher risk of losing its viability than in periods of balanced growth, when the stakes are not as high. For example, when a leap in growth occurs for a limited time (through external factors such as deregulation or new developments in technology, or through internal factors such as changes in top management or a merger and acquisition), leaders need to offset that growth by intentionally introducing balancing feedback loops. They can do so through control and coordination systems as well as through productivity enhancement programs. These loops keep the organization's growth from consuming the company.

7.3.5 Leadership in organizational evolution

But how can leaders help firms achieve the balanced growth they need to evolve? Through strategic management, leaders expand the business; through management control, they regulate the growth process, making sure that it remains within a sustainable range. Together, the two functions form a balanced leadership cycle for guiding and controlling the company's evolution.

7.3.6 Strategic management

Through strategic management, leaders cultivate the conditions for a company's sustainable growth. Specifically, they perform the following three functions:

1. *Set direction*. As mentioned earlier, leaders need to preserve or redefine the organization's core identity and develop its structures in ways that lead to lasting success. They do so by communicating the company's values and beliefs to employees and external stakeholders through shared vision and mission statements, and by strengthening internal reinforcing processes such as employee morale. They also formulate and implement strategy, not by detailing a map of action but rather by defining a corridor of learning opportunities.
2. *Build resources*. Leaders need resources to support entrepreneurial activity. They can acquire them externally (such as machinery or capital) or develop them internally (such as people or policies). From a resource-based perspective, only internally built resources can provide the basis for competitive advantages and above average returns, because they are specific to the company and therefore more difficult to imitate. On the other hand, resources that are available on the open market are available to all competitors.
3. *Create infrastructure*. Leaders must not attempt to drive growth but rather to influence the factors that can block or support it. As such, they need to design an organizational context that

eliminates barriers to company development (such as fear, distrust, centralized decision making, too-tight control, and insufficient resources) and develop processes to promote learning (such as organizing flexible teams, supporting communities of practice, creating incentive systems for transferring knowledge, and creating learning spaces). From a system dynamics perspective, these three functions combine to form a reinforcing process called the "Strategic management Loop", which strengthens the company's growth. But for the organization to remain viable, this reinforcing loop must be reined in by balancing processes, such as those that make up the "Management Control Loop".

7.3.7 Management control

Management control acts to bring equilibrium to the expanding system. To do so, leaders must perform three central functions:

1. *Assure internal consistency of infrastructure, resources, and direction.*
   Leaders need to maintain the coherence of a system, particularly in large companies where management functions often get split among different organizational units or departments. To handle this specialization of functions, they must synchronize the development of strategy, resources, structure, and systems. They do so by working with others to develop a shared view of the system, which acts as a basis of companywide activity. However, this model is necessarily a subjective simplification of complex reality, so it can easily become selective and distorted.
2. *Compensate for selective perception.* Therefore, leaders and their teams must compensate for their selective perception by continually enriching their assumptions with relevant new information and challenging their mental models. For example, they might use management information and decision support systems, which provide comprehensive data and make blind spots of organizational perception visible. Management control thus leads to more informed decision making and better anticipation of the consequences of those decisions.
3. *Appropriately limit developmental dynamics.* Designing appropriate limits on developmental dynamics involves two realms: content and time. Leaders must analyse whether the firm's expansion exceeds the limits set by its internal conditions (for instance, the number of staff with expertise in certain areas) and the external forces of its environment (for example, the size of the market), thus endangering its boundaries. They also must regulate how fast the firm grows. They do so by pacing the speed of growth so it does not overtax the current management capacity (resources and

infrastructure) or environmental limits (size and growth of the market). Leaders put these functions into action using different diagnostic tools, such as the balanced scorecard and budgeting. The balanced scorecard helps them to see the interconnections among the key measures of the business, for instance, between employee capacity and customer satisfaction, or between customer satisfaction and market share. Executives can then ensure that key measures stay in balance. Through the budgeting process, they translate strategic direction into financial objectives, setting the framework for the allocation of resources and the utilization of infrastructures to assure internal consistency. By limiting and balancing developmental dynamics as well as by assuring internal consistency, these tools contribute to the fulfilment of the management control function in the balanced leadership cycle. In order to avoid survival threatening oscillations between growth and decline, leaders need to take into account the time delays that occur before balancing impulses take effect. Working properly, the interplay of strategic management (growth actions) and management control (balancing impulses) assures a synergistic rhythm of a company's evolution, a characteristic of particularly successful firms in dynamic environments.

7.3.8 Next steps

1. *Shift your thinking* from regarding your organization as a *machine* that you have to maintain by fixing small problems to regarding it as a *living system* that you must nurture by enhancing its capacity for learning and sustainable growth.
2. *Design and implement a strategic management infrastructure* that follows the principles of viable systems by preserving or redefining the organization's core identity and by influencing the factors that can block or support organizational learning.
3. *Design and implement a management control infrastructure that follow* the principles of viable systems by regulating the growth process appropriately so that the company's expansion remains within a sustainable range.
4. *Use tools like mission statements, scenario planning, causal loop diagrams, and the balanced scorecard* to support the dynamic interplay of strategic management and management control to lead your organization to evolve successfully.

7.4 Essay No. 4: Team building without time wasting

This essay material is reproduced with permission from Dr Marshall Goldsmi°th and Howard Morgan; this article was originally published in Leader Values, 1998, and is produced with permission. © Keilty, Goldsmith & Company. All rights reserved.

7.4.1 Introduction

Teams seem to be becoming more and more common and important. Management theorists and organizations around the world are extolling the value of teamwork. As the traditional, hierarchical school of leadership begins to diminish in significance, a new focus on networked team leadership is emerging to take its place. Leaders are finding themselves as members of all kinds of teams, including virtual teams, autonomous teams, cross-functional teams, and action learning teams.

Many of today's leaders face a dilemma, as the *need* to build effective teams is increasing; the available *time* to build these teams is often decreasing. A common challenge faced by today's leaders is the necessity of building teams in an environment of rapid change with limited resources. The process of reengineering and streamlining, when coupled with increased demand for services, has led to a situation where most leaders feel that they have more work to do and fewer staff members to help them do it.

Research involving thousands of participants has shown how focussed feedback and follow-up can increase leadership and customer service effectiveness. (1) A parallel approach to team building has been shown to help leaders build teamwork without wasting time. While the approach described will be simple, it will not be easy. It will require that team members have the courage to regularly ask for feedback and the discipline to develop a behavioural change strategy, to follow-up, and to "stick with it".

To successfully implement the following team-building process, the leader will need to assume the role of coach or facilitator, and fight the urge to be the "boss" of the project. Greater improvement in teamwork will generally occur if the team members develop their own behavioural change strategy than will occur if the leader develops the strategy and imposes it on the team. This process should not be implemented if the leader has the present intention of firing or removing a team member.

7.4.2 Steps in the process

Begin by asking individual members of the team to confidentially record their individual answers to two questions: (a) "On a 1–10 scale (with 10 being ideal) how well are we doing in terms of working together as a team?" and (b) "On a 1–10 scale how well do we need to do in terms of working together as a team?"

Before beginning a team-building process, it is important to determine if the team feels that team building is both important and needed. Some groups of people report to the same manager, but legitimately may have very little reason to work interactively as a team. Other groups may believe that teamwork is important, but feel that the team is already functioning smoothly and that a team-building activity would be a waste of time.

Have a team member to calculate the results. Discuss the results with the team. If the team members believe that the gap between current effectiveness and needed effectiveness indicates the need for team building, proceed to the next step in the process.

In most cases, team members do believe that improved teamwork is both important and needed. Recent interviews involving members from several hundred teams (in multinational corporations) showed that the "average" team member believed that his or her team was currently at a "5.8" level of effectiveness but needed to be at an "8.7".

Ask the team, "If every team member could change two key behaviours which would help us close the gap between where we are and where we want to be, which two behaviours we all should try to change?" Have each team member recorded their selected behaviours on flip charts?

Help team members to prioritize all the behaviours on the charts (many will be the same or similar) and (using consensus) determine the two most important behaviours to change (for all team members).

Have each team member has a one-on-one dialogue with each other team member. During the dialogue, individual members will request that their colleague suggest two areas for personal behavioural change (other than the two already agreed upon for every team member) that will help the team to close the gap between where we are and where we want to be.

These dialogues occur simultaneously and take about 5 min each. For example, if there are seven team members, each team member will participate in six brief one-on-one dialogues.

Let each team member review his or her list of suggested behavioural changes and choose the two that seem to be the most important. Let each team member then announce the two key behaviours for personal change to the team.

Encourage each team member to ask for a brief (5 min), monthly "progress report" from each other team member on the effectiveness in demonstrating the two key behaviours common to all team members and the two key personal behaviours. Specific suggestions for improvement can be solicited in areas where behaviour does not match desired expectations.

Conduct a minisurvey follow-up process in approximately 4 months. In the minisurvey, each team member will receive confidential feedback from all other team members on his or her perceived change in effectiveness. This survey will include two common items, the two personal items, and an item that assesses how much the individual has been following up with the other team members. The minisurveys are simple enough to be put on a postcard and might look as follows:

It has an outside supplier to calculate the results for each individual (on all items) and calculate the summary results for all team members (on the common team items). Each team member can then receive a confidential summary report indicating the degree to which colleagues see his or her increased effectiveness in demonstrating the desired behaviours. Each member can also receive a summary report on the team's progress on the items selected for all team members.

"Before and after" studies have clearly shown that if team members have regularly followed-up with their colleagues, they will almost invariably be seen as increasing their effectiveness in their selected individual "areas for improvement". The group summary will also tend to show that (overall) team members will have increased in effectiveness on the common team items. The minisurvey summary report will give team members a chance to get positive reinforcement for improvement (and to learn what has not improved) after a reasonably short period of time. The minisurvey will also help to validate the importance of "sticking with it" and "following-up".

In a team meeting, have each team member discuss key learnings from their minisurvey results and ask for further suggestions in a brief one-on-one dialogue with each other team member? Review the summary results with the team. Facilitate a discussion on how the team (as a whole) is doing in terms of increasing its effectiveness in the two key behaviours that were selected for all team members. Provide the team with positive recognition for increased effectiveness in teamwork. Encourage team members to keep focussed on increasing their effectiveness in demonstrating the behaviours that that they are trying to improve.

Have each team member continue to conduct his or her brief monthly "progress report" sessions with each other team member. Readminister the minisurvey (in 4 month intervals) after 8 months from the beginning of the process and again after 1 year.

Conduct a summary session with the team 1 year after the process has started. Review the results of the final minisurvey and ask the team members to rate the team's effectiveness on where we are vs where we need to be in terms of working together as a team. Compare these ratings with the original ratings that were calculated one year earlier. (If team members followed the process in a reasonably disciplined fashion, the team will almost always see a dramatic improvement in teamwork.) Give the team positive recognition for improvement in teamwork and have each team member (in a brief one-on-one dialogue) to recognize each of his or her colleagues for improvements in behaviour that have occurred over the past 12 months.

Ask the team if they believe that more work on team building will be needed in the upcoming year. If the team believes that more work would be beneficial, continue the process. If the team believes that more work is not needed "declare victory" and work on something else.

7.4.3 Why this process works

The process described above works because it is highly focussed, includes disciplined feedback and follow-up, does not waste time, and causes participants to focus on self-improvement. Most survey feedback processes ask respondents to complete too many items. In such surveys, most of the items never result in any behavioural change and participants feel that they are wasting time. Participants almost never object to completing four-item surveys that are specifically designed to fit each team member's unique needs. The process also works because it provides ongoing feedback and reinforcement. Most survey processes provide participants with feedback every 12–24 months. Any research on behavioural change will show that feedback and reinforcement for new behaviour needs to occur much more frequently than a yearly or biyearly review. A final reason that the process works is because it encourages participants to focus on self-improvement. Many team-building processes degenerate because team members are primarily focussed on solving *someone else's* problems. This process works because it encourages team members to primarily focus on solving *their own* problems.

Let me close with a challenge to you (the reader) as a team leader. Try it! The "downside" is very low. The process takes very little time and the first minisurvey will show very quickly if progress is being made. The "upside" can be very high. As effective teamwork becomes more and more important, the brief amount of time that you invest in this process may produce a great return for your team and an even greater return for your organization.

7.5 Essay No. 5: Distinguishing teams from work groups is critical

This essay material is reproduced with permission from Marie J. Kane, President Executive Evolution, Publisher http://www.Executive Evolution.com, 2001.

7.5.1 Introduction

Before you embark on any kind of team development, it is critical that you understand the implications of the differences between teams and work groups.

Is your group a real team or a work group or something in between now and what does it need to be for your situation? How you approach that development of your team or group will differ depending on the nature of the group, its mission and what therefore they must address to operate effectively. A group's understanding and application of this difference significantly enhances its developmental process. A group needs to establish what kind of group it is presently and what kind of group it aspires to be or to maintain.

Jon R. Katzenbach and Douglas K. Smith in their 1993 book "The Wisdom of Teams" provide excellent, very usable distinctions among the kinds of groups currently operating in organizations.

7.5.2 Team, work group, or neither?

Working group: No significant incremental performance need or opportunity that would require it to become a team. The members interact primarily to share information, best practices, or perspectives and to make decisions to help each individual perform within his or her area of responsibility. There is no call for either a team approach or a mutual accountability requirement.

Pseudoteam: This is a group for which there could be a significant, incremental performance need or opportunity, but it has not focussed on collective performance and is not really trying to achieve it. It has no interest in shaping a common purpose or set of performance goals, even though it may call itself a team. Pseudoteams are the weakest of all groups in terms of performance impact. In pseudoteams, the sum of the whole is less than the potential of the individual parts. They almost always contribute less to company performance needs than working groups because their interactions detract from each member's individual performance without delivering any joint benefits. For a pseudoteam, to have the option of becoming a potential team, the group must define goals so it has something concrete to do as a team that is a valuable contribution to the company.

Potential team: There is a significant, incremental performance need, and it really is trying to improve its performance impact. Typically it requires more clarity about purpose, goals, or work products and more discipline in hammering out a common working approach. It has not yet established collective accountability. Potential teams abound in organizations. When a team (as opposed to a working group) approach makes sense, the performance impact can be high. The steepest performance gain comes between a potential team and a real team; but any movement up the slope is worth pursuing.

Real team: This is a small number of people with complementary skills who are equally committed to a common purpose, goals, and working approach for which they hold themselves mutually accountable. Real teams are a basic unit of performance. The possible performance impact for the real team is significantly higher than the working group.

High-performance team: This is a group that meets all the conditions of real teams and has embers who are also deeply committed to one another's personal growth and success. That commitment usually transcends the team. The high-performance team significantly outperforms all other like teams, and outperforms all reasonable expectations given its membership. It is a powerful possibility and an excellent model for all real and potential teams.

Definitions used in the TEAMS manual (Executive Evolution's team survey, team development and continuous improvement process) with permission from Harvard Business School Press, from "Wisdom of Teams" by Jon R. Katzenbach and Douglas K. Smith, Copyright 1993.

These distinctions between a team and a work group are very important because the operating level of a group effects:

1. The ability of groups of people to contribute to their organization
2. The levels of personal growth and satisfaction of group members
3. The return on resources (time, talent, money, etc.) expended by the group
4. The requirements for operating, growing and maintaining the group.

The difference between a work group and a real team

A careful study of the preceding definitions reveals fundamental factors that distinguish between work groups and real teams. These factors are the presence or absence of:

- An incremental performance need or opportunity
- True interdependence
- Real shared accountability.

The best single criterion to use for determining whether a team or a work group is the best choice for a given situation is this: does an incremental performance need or opportunity exist? Put another way, is there a need or opportunity to make a significant difference in organizational performance? It is important to select the right kind of group, either work group or team, for each situation. One is not inherently better than the other. If a significant performance need or opportunity exists, then a team is potentially a better choice. If it does not, then a work group is preferable. Teams have greater performance potential, but require more development and maintenance than work groups. It comes down to an issue of return on investment. Remember also that return is measured not only in dollars, but in quality of work life and other intangibles, which will ultimately, though not always immediately, effect the bottom line.

Examples of situations where real teams are needed are sports teams or emergency room trauma teams. For both of these, there is a key performance need or opportunity, true interdependency, and shared accountability. If they are not functioning as real teams, the result is a disaster.

Examples of situations where you often find work groups are a functional department in an organization, clerks in a department store, or waiters in a restaurant. In each one of these groups, there can be similar individual objectives but a lack of any small group common objective. There is some form of coordination or collaboration, but not usually shared accountability or interdependency. In each of these work group examples, if a significant performance need or opportunity existed, then it would be worthwhile to explore the choice to become a real team with a common group objective, shared accountability, true interdependency and other real team attributes.

The decision whether to become a real team or a work group should be made based on the advantages obtained versus the investment required.

In organizations, we might also find pseudoteams, potential teams, and high-performance teams as described in the definitions above. Because of the many benefits that high-performance teams bring to the organization, it is desirable to encourage and nurture them where they exist to serve a significant perfor ance opportunity. Potential teams should be assisted to move toward real team functioning, since, by definition, an incremental performance need or opportunity exists. Pseudoteams are very expensive to an organization because they consume resources without a commensurate return. A pseudoteam is better off moving toward either becoming a team or becoming a work group, whichever is most appropriate for the specific situation. For any of these changes to take place, it is necessary first to determine what the current status of the group is with respect to the possible kinds of groups that have been defined.

7.5.3 Importance of how to determine kind of group

This is a very important discussion, because it touches on the core of how group members see themselves collectively, and of what they are potentially capable. If a group or the organization's management has a blind spot about the kind of group it is, or simply fails to recognize this as an issue, there are significant consequences. In this situation, the group:

1. Cannot determine whether they are properly organized to accomplish what the organization needs from them
2. Cannot correctly assess their performance potential
3. Cannot choose the appropriate strategies to manage or grow the group.

If it is not already clearly established what the current status of the group is, and what it aspires to be, then it is important to guide the group through a discussion on this subject. One helpful approach is to list on a flip chart the following character-istics, explain them to the group and then attain a group consen-sus on the degree to which they apply for that group. Record for each characteristic the group's conclusion about the degree to which that characteristic applies to them. A scale from "totally" to "not at all" (6 to 1) would be appropriate as a measurement scale.

7.5.3.1 Characteristics list

1. There is a significant incremental performance need or opportunity
2. There is joint commitment to a common mission
3. There is consensus on objectives
4. There is agreement on working approach
5. There is true interdependency
6. There is mutual accountability
7. Members are committed to one another's personal growth and success
8. We outperform other like teams and outperform perform-ance expectations.

Based on the discussion, determine what this group is. If item 1 does not apply, then the group needs to look at being a work group or something else, not a real team. If items 1–6 "all" apply, it is a team. If only some of these items are true, then it may be a potential team. If items 1–8 all apply, then it is a high-perform-ance team. The group must determine through discussion on these criteria both what it is and what it needs to be.

Finally, it is worth mentioning that some models suggest that only cross-functional groups can be teams. I do not support that view. Whether or not you are a real team depends upon the presence of an incremental performance need or opportunity, true interdependence, and shared accountability, not cross-func-tionality per se. You do not have to be a cross-functional group to be a real team. What is true, is that many incremental per-formance needs or opportunities require a cross-functional team approach to be addressed effectively. It is also helpful to remem-ber that, while complimentarily of skills among team members may refer to differences in technical or functional skills that are job related (examples: marketing, engineering, computer tech-nology), it can also refer to differences in more generically appli-cable skills such as problem-solving, decision-making and interpersonal skills.

It is also worth mentioning that the length of time a group will be in existence, or the permanency of its charter, are not generally appropriate criteria to determine its current or future status unless the time frame is so short that it would be impossible to create a real team. Short- and long-term groups, permanent or semi-permanent (membership may change) groups or temporary groups can be either teams or work groups.

In summary, one of the most powerful actions a group can take on behalf of itself and the organization is to determine what kind of group it currently is and what kind it needs to be to best serve the needs of the organization and its employees. This is a very powerful step in the group's development. Then the group can proceed with appropriate planning for its own development in concert with what the organization needs it to be and with an appropriate investment of developmental resources for the possible return.

7.6 Biographies

7.6.1 Essay No. 1: Paul Tarplett

Paul Tarplett is the Director, National and Local Services. Paul leads OPM's work with local, regional, and national government. He manages large-scale organizational change projects, particularly focussing on performance management and culture change; designs and delivers management and leadership development programmes for a wide range of clients; carries out senior team development; supports government bodies implementing policy or project initiatives; and provides executive coaching for clients across the public sector. Before joining OPM, Paul held posts in large private companies as head of human resources and as training and development manager. Earlier in his career, Paul was both a lecturer and a manager in further education and worked for BTEC, where he led the evaluation and redesign of the national curriculum in business and management.

7.6.2 Essay No. 2: Dr David Gould

Dave is currently the Campus Department Chair for Information Systems and Technology at the University of Phoenix, Washington (Seattle) Campus. He graduated from Seattle University in 1997 with a Doctor in Education (Educational Leadership). Dave's previous education included a BA in Mathematics, an MBA, and a Master's in Software Engineering.

7.6.3 Essay No. 3: Dr Stafan C Gueldenberg and Dr Werner Hoffmann

Stefan C. Gueldenberg, PhD, is an assistant professor at the Department for Strategic Management, Management Control and Consulting, Vienna University of Economics and Business Administration. He is an expert in using systems thinking to facilitate organizational learning and has published numerous articles on this subject.

Dr Werner H. Hoffmann is an associate professor for strategic management at Vienna University of Economics and Business Administration, and founder and president of Contrast Management Consulting. His research focuses on leadership, evolutionary theory, and strategic alliances.

7.6.4 Essay No. 4: Dr Marshall Goldsmith and Howard Morgan

Dr Marshall Goldsmith is a founding director of A4SL – The Alliance for Strategic Leadership, a consulting alliance that includes over 200 top professionals in the field of leadership development. He is also the cofounder of the Financial Times Knowledge Dialogue, a videoconference network that connects executives with the world's greatest thinkers. He has a PhD from UCLA. He is the faculty of the global executive education program for Dartmouth, Michigan, and Oxford (UK) Universities. Marshall has partnerships with Hewitt Associates and Russell Reynolds to provide coaching for leaders around the globe. He has served on the Board of the Peter Drucker Foundation for 10 years.

Howard Morgan is the founder of 50 Top Coaches, a collective of many of the world's leading executive advisors. He specializes in coaching as a strategic change-management tool. He is coeditor of the book "The Art and Practice of Leadership Coaching: 50 Top Executive Coaches Reveal Their Secrets" (John Wiley & Sons, December 2004).

7.6.5 Essay No. 5: Marie J. Kane

Marie Kane is the President of Executive Evolution. Since 1981, Marie has provided executive consulting and coaching services to help clients develop and implement the right strategy, leverage the company's human talent, and create optimal culture and communication. Her services include leadership, executive, management and team development, strategic and operational planning, employee selection, retention and development, change management, conflict resolution, and a variety of profiles and assessments, including 360's.

Marie may be reached at *Marie@ExecutiveEvolution.com* or through her website http://*www.executiveevolution.com*.

Appendix A: Examples of Professional Codes of Ethics

Project Management Institute (PMI)

The Project Management Institute (PMI) has taken an additional step and tied ethical standards to certification requirements for its certified Project Management Professionals (PMPs) worldwide. The association maintains two codes of ethics – one for PMI members and one for its certified PMPs. Candidates for certification must agree to adhere to PMI's code of ethics, even if they are not PMI members. According to the PMI's code, Project Management Professionals, in the pursuit of the profession, affect the quality of life of all people in our society. Therefore, it is vital that Project Management Professionals conduct their work in an ethical manner to earn and maintain the confidence of team members, colleagues, employees, employers, clients, and the public.

Project management professional code of professional conduct

I Responsibilities to the profession

(A) Compliance with all organizational rules and policies

1. Provide accurate and truthful representations concerning all information directly or indirectly related to all aspects of the PMI Certification Program, including and not limited to the following: examination applications, test item banks, examinations, answer sheets, candidate information, and professional development program reporting forms.
2. Upon a reasonable and clear factual basis, report possible violations of the professional code of conduct by individuals in the field of project management.

3. Cooperate with PMI concerning ethics violations and the collection of related information.
4. Disclose to clients, customers, owners, or contractors, significant circumstances that could be construed as a conflict of interest, or an appearance of impropriety.

(B) Candidate/certificated professional practice

1. Provide accurate, truthful advertising/representations concerning qualifications, experience and performance of services.
2. Comply with laws, regulations, and ethical standards governing professional practice in the state/province and/or country when providing project management services.

(C) Advancement of the profession

1. Recognize and respect intellectual property developed or owned by others, and otherwise act in accurate, truthful, and complete manner, including all activities related to professional work and research.
2. Support and disseminate the professional code of conduct to other PMI certificants.

II Candidate/certificants responsibilities to customers and the public

(A) Qualifications, experience, and performance of professional services

1. Provide accurate and truthful representations to the public in advertising, public statements, and in the preparation of estimates concerning costs, services, and expected results.
2. Maintain and satisfy the scope and objectives of professional services, unless otherwise directed by the customer.
3. Maintain and respect the confidentiality of sensitive information obtained in the course of professional activities or otherwise where a clear obligation exists.

(B) Conflict of interest situations and other prohibited professional conduct

1. Ensure that a conflict of interest does not compromise legitimate interests of a client or customer, or influence/interfere with professional judgments.
2. Refrain from offering or accepting inappropriate payments, gifts, or other forms of compensation for personal gain, unless

in conformity with applicable laws or customs of the country where project management services are being provided.

PMI®, PMBOK®, Project Management Institute®, and "Building professionalism in project management®." are federally registered trademarks of the Project Management Institute, Inc. PMP® and Project Management Professional® are federally registered certification marks of the Project Management Institute, Inc.

British Computer Society (BCS)

British computer society code of professional conduct (version 2.0)

Introduction

This code sets out the professional standards required by the Society as a condition of membership. It applies to members of all grades, including students, and affiliates, and also non-members who offer their expertise as part of the Society's Professional Advice Register. Within this document, the term *relevant authority* is used to identify the person or organization, which has authority over your activity as an individual. If you are a practising professional, this is normally an employer or client. If you are a student, this is normally an academic institution.

The code governs your personal conduct as an individual member of the BCS and not the nature of business or ethics of the relevant authority. It will, therefore, be a matter of your exercising your personal judgement in meeting the code's requirements. Any breach of the Code of Conduct brought to the attention of the Society will be considered under the Society's disciplinary procedures. You should also ensure that you notify the Society of any significant violation of this code by another BCS member.

The public interest

1. You shall carry out work or study with due care and diligence in accordance with the relevant authority's requirements, and the interests of system users. If your professional judgement is overruled, you shall indicate the likely risks and consequences.
   - The crux of the issue here, familiar to all professionals in whatever field, is the potential conflict between full

and committed compliance with the relevant authority's wishes, and the independent and considered exercise of your judgment.

- If your judgment is overruled, you are encouraged to seek advice and guidance from a peer or colleague on how best to respond.

2. In your professional role you shall have regard for the public health, safety, and environment.
   - This is a general responsibility, which may be governed by legislation, convention, or protocol.
   - If in doubt over the appropriate course of action to take in particular circumstances, you should seek the counsel of a peer or colleague.

3. You shall have regard to the legitimate rights of third parties.
   - The term *third party* includes professional colleagues, or possibly competitors, or members of "the public" who might be affected by an IS project without their being directly aware of its existence.

4. You shall ensure that within your professional field/s you have knowledge and understanding of relevant legislation, regulations and standards, and that you comply with such requirements.
   - As examples, relevant legislation could, in the UK, include the UK Public Disclosure Act, Data Protection or Privacy legislation, Computer Misuse law, legislation concerned with the export or import of technology, possibly for national security reasons, or law relating to intellectual property. This list is not exhaustive, and you should ensure that you are aware of any legislation relevant to your professional responsibilities.
   - In the international context, you should be aware of, and understand, the requirements of law specific to the jurisdiction within which you are working, and where relevant, to supranational legislation such as EU law and regulation. You should seek specialist advice when necessary.

5. You shall conduct your professional activities without discrimination against clients or colleagues
   - Grounds of discrimination include race, colour, ethnic origin, sexual orientation.
   - All colleagues have a right to be treated with dignity and respect.
   - You should adhere to relevant law within the jurisdiction where you are working and, if appropriate, the European Convention on Human Rights.

- You are encouraged to promote equal access to the benefits of IS by all groups in society, and to avoid and reduce "social exclusion" from IS wherever opportunities arise.

6. You shall reject any offer of bribery or inducement.

Duty to relevant authority

7. You shall avoid any situation that may give rise to a conflict of interest between you and your relevant authority. You shall make full and immediate disclosure to them if any conflict is likely to occur or be seen by a third party as likely to occur.

8. You shall not disclose or authorize to be disclosed, or use for personal gain or to benefit a third party, confidential information except with the permission of your relevant authority, or at the direction of a court of law.

9. You shall not misrepresent or withhold information on the performance of products, systems or services, or take advantage of the lack of relevant knowledge or inexperience of others.

Duty to the profession

10. You shall uphold the reputation and good standing of the BCS in particular, and the profession in general, and shall seek to improve professional standards through participation in their development, use, and enforcement.

    - As a Member of the BCS you also have a wider responsibility to promote public understanding of IS – its benefits and pitfalls – and, whenever practical, to counter misinformation that brings or could bring the profession into disrepute.

    - You should encourage and support fellow members in their professional development and, where possible, provide opportunities for the professional development of new members, particularly student members. Enlightened mutual assistance between IS professionals furthers the reputation of the profession, and assists individual members.

11. You shall act with integrity in your relationships with all members of the BCS and with members of other professions with whom you work in a professional capacity.

12. You shall have due regard for the possible consequences of your statements on others. You shall not make any public statement in your professional capacity unless you are properly qualified and, where appropriate, authorized to do so. You shall not purport to represent the BCS unless authorized to do so.

- The offering of an opinion in public, holding oneself out to be an expert in the subject in question, is a major personal responsibility and should not be undertaken lightly.
- To give an opinion that subsequently proves ill founded is a disservice to the profession and to the BCS.

13. You shall notify the Society if convicted of a criminal offence or upon becoming bankrupt or disqualified as Company Director.

Professional competence and integrity

14. You shall seek to upgrade your professional knowledge and skill, and shall maintain awareness of technological developments, procedures, and standards which are relevant to your field, and encourage your subordinates to do likewise.
15. You shall not claim any level of competence that you do not possess. You shall only offer to do work or provide a service that is within your professional competence.
    - You can self-assess your professional competence for undertaking a particular job or role by asking, for example,
      (i) Am I familiar with the technology involved, or have I worked with similar technology before?
      (ii) Have I successfully completed similar assignments or roles in the past?
      (iii) Can I demonstrate adequate knowledge of the specific business application and requirements successfully to undertake the work?
16. You shall observe the relevant BCS Codes of Practice and all other standards, which in your judgement, are relevant, and you shall encourage your colleagues to do likewise.
17. You shall accept professional responsibility for your work and for the work of colleagues who are defined in a given context as working under your supervision.

The British Computer Society, 1 Sanford Street, Swindon SN1 1HJ

Email: bcshq@hq.bcs.org.uk Website: www.bcs.org

The BCS is a member of the Council of European Professional Informatics Societies (CEPIS). The BCS is a Registered Charity: Number 292786. ©British Computer Society 2005.

Reproduced with permission of the BCS, 2005.

Glossary of Terms

Accountability   The capacity to account for one's actions or as a representative of an organization, to account for either individual's actions or the actions of the organization. The term is usually used in the voluntary sector to refer to the responsibility a nonprofit organization has to inform donors of the manner in which their gifts were used.

Adaptive leadership   In adaptive situations, the organization must constantly sense changes in the external environment and then respond to these changes – rather than sticking to a well worn and preplanned path. Adaptive leaders must thus help their organizations change in ways that will allow it to do what it has never done before. An adaptive leader must therefore manage patterns, paradox, transformation and actions, rather than predicting and controlling people and events.

Affirmative action   Any action intended to correct effects of past discrimination, eliminate present discrimination, or prevent discrimination in the future.

Assumptions list   A document that briefly lists any assumptions on which a given and chosen option was based.

Attitude   The way a person views a situation or a condition and then behaves accordingly. This is an important consideration in team building.

Attributes   Characteristics, qualities, or properties, attributes of the leader fall into three categories: mental, physical, and emotional.

Audit   The systematic examination of records and documents to determine compliance with specified standards and policy.

Authority   The legitimate power given to a person in an organization to use resources to reach an objective and to exercise discipline.

Behavioural theories Leadership theories that identified behaviours, which differentiated effective leaders from ineffective leaders.

Beliefs Assumptions and convictions that a person holds to be true regarding people, concepts, or things.

Brainstorming A technique for teams that is used to generate ideas on a subject. Each person on the team is asked to think creatively and write down as many ideas as possible. After the writing session, the ideas are discussed by the team.

Building An activity focussed on sustaining and renewing the organization. It involves actions that indicate commitment to the achievement of group or organizational goals: timely and effective discharge of operational and organizational duties and obligations; working effectively with others; compliance with and active support of organizational goals, rules, and policies.

Business The techniques and expertise of setting strategies, efficient organization, planning, direction, and control of operations to meet specific goals and to reward stakeholders, employees, stockholders, etc. and activities involving the exchange of money for goods or services.

Change management An organized, systematic application of the knowledge, tools, and resources of change that provides organizations with a key process to achieve goals and objectives.

Character The sum total of an individual's personality traits and the link between individual's values and behaviour.

Climate A short-term phenomenon created by the current junior or senior leaders. Organizational climate is a system of the perception of people about the organization and its leaders, directly attributed to the leadership and management style of the leaders based on the skills, knowledge, attitude, and priorities of the leaders. The personality and behaviour of the - leaders creates a climate that influences everyone in the organization.

Coaching A method of knowledge distribution with the objective of deepening learning and improving performance. The coach is usually not an employee of the organization but an outside consultant.

Coalition An alliance of individuals or organizations working together in a common effort for a common purpose to make more effective and efficient use of resources.

Coercive power   The power the leaders have because of their ability to punish or control.

Commitment   An obligation, pledge, or promise by an organization to its stakeholders, and an expression of support through dedication as a contributor or volunteer worker.

Communicating   Comprises the ability to express oneself effectively in individual and group situations either orally or in writing. It involves a sender transmitting an idea to a receiver.

Company or corporation   A legally defined business entity separate from its owners. It lives on independent of the original owners or employees. It can own assets. It can sue and be sued in the courts. The legal requirements and limitations regarding the setting up of a company or corporation are determined by company law. This also provides the entity with limited liability.

Conflict   A struggle resulting from incompatible or opposing desires.

Conflict of interest   Any business activity, personal or company related, that interferes with the company's goals or that entails unethical or illegal actions.

Consensus   In decision making, full agreement within the group of a course of action including all its details. This approach requires negotiation within the group of all the precise details. While leading to a higher level of "buy-in", the result tends to be equivalent to the "lowest" common denominator. Negotiations may be protracted and the final course not necessarily optimal and in the best interests of the project goals.

Constraint   Any element or factor that prevents individuals from reaching a higher level of performance with respect to their goal.

Core competency   Fundamental knowledge, ability, or expertise in a specific subject area or skill set. To be considered a core competency, a capability must be an essential part of an organization's offerings and it must describe a significant advantage in the marketplace.

Corrective action   The implementation of solutions resulting in the reduction or elimination of an identified problem.

Courage   The virtue that enables us to conquer fear, danger, or adversity, no matter what the context happens to be (physical or moral). Courage includes the notion of taking responsibility for decisions and actions. Additionally, the idea involves the ability to perform critical self-assessment, confront new ideas, and change.

Credibility   The degree to which followers perceive someone as honest, competent, and able to inspire.

Culture   The long-term complex phenomenon that can be affected by strategic leaders. Culture represents the shared expectations and self-image of the organization. The mature values that create "tradition", the play out of "climate", or "the feel of the organization" over time, and the deep, unwritten code that frames "how we do things around here" contribute to the culture. Organizational culture is a system of shared values, assumptions, beliefs, and norms that unite the members of the organization. Individual leaders cannot easily create or change culture.

Customer or client   The person served by an organization.

Decision making   The process of reaching logical conclusions, solving problems, analysing factual information, and taking appropriate actions based on the conclusions.

Delegate leadership   A style of leadership in which the leader entrusts decision making to an employee, and the leader is still responsible for their decisions.

Democratic style   A leader who tends to involve employees in decision making, delegate authority, encourage participation in deciding work methods, and uses feedback as an opportunity for coaching employees.

Desired outcomes   The results or products that a training programme, process, instructional unit, or learning activity strives to achieve as defined in measurable terms.

Developing   The art of developing the competence and confidence of subordinate leaders through role modelling and training and development activities related to their current or future duties.

Effectiveness   The extent to which a programme has made desired changes or met its goals and objectives through the delivery of services. Effectiveness can be judged in terms of both input and output.

Efficiency   A measure (as a percentage) of the actual output to the standard output expected. Efficiency measures how well someone is performing relative to expectations.

Empowerment   Technically, a condition whereby employees have the authority to make decisions and take action in their work areas, jobs, or tasks without prior approval. It allows the employees the responsibility normally associated with leaders. Empowerment is a "deal" between the leader and his or her followers. The followers and the leader have an agreement for success and failure, reward and sanction on both sides. Both are given mutual freedom, yet held mutually accountable. Both are thus empowered.

Ethics   The moral considerations of the activities of an organization or a system or code of conduct that is based on universal moral duties and obligations that indicate how one should behave. It deals with the ability to distinguish good from evil, right from wrong, and propriety from impropriety.

External environment   The prevailing conditions in the country or region that affect programme development, including culture, policy, economy, health, and market; sources of funding and commodities; and demographics.

Governance   The structure and policies for decision making, which include board, staff, and constituents. Governance, in the nonprofit sector, refers to the actions of the board of directors of an organization with respect to establishing and monitoring the long-term direction of that organization.

Group dynamics   Understanding the relationships among people in groups and how groups begin, operate, and end.

Influencing   The key feature of leadership, performed through communicating, decision making, and motivating.

Integrity   A moral virtue that encompasses the sum of a person's set of values and moral code. A breach of any of these values will damage the integrity of the individual. Integrity comes from the same Latin root (integritas) as the word *integer*, refers to a notion of completeness, wholeness, and uniqueness. Integrity also entails the consistent adherence of action to one's personal moral beliefs.

Leader–member relations   One of Fiedler's situational contingencies that describe the degree of confidence, trust, and respect employees have for their leader.

Leader participation model   A leadership contingency model that related leadership behaviour and participation in decision making.

Leadership   The energetic process of getting other people fully and willingly committed to a new course of action to meet commonly agreed objectives whilst having commonly held values.

Leadership goal   Anything that, by virtue of its achievement, will place an organization in a leadership position among similar organizations.

Learning organization   An organization that looks for meaningful solutions, then internalizes those solutions so that they continue to grow, develop, and remain successful. Learning organizations incorporate ideas from many sources and involve a variety of people in problem solving, information sharing, and celebrating success.

Legitimacy   The perceived fairness of a dispute resolution process. Legitimacy of decision-making procedures is important, because illegitimate procedures almost always escalate conflicts making their ultimate resolution more difficult.

Lessons learned   The process of discovering what happened and why, through evaluation, then applying what is learned to improve performance in the future.

Loyalty   The intangible bond based on a legitimate obligation; it entails the correct ordering of our obligations and commitments. Loyalty demands commitment to the organization and is a precondition for trust, cooperation, teamwork, and camaraderie.

Management by objectives (MBO)   A participative goal-setting process that enables the manager or supervisor to construct and communicate the goals of the department to each subordinate. At the same time, the subordinate is able to formulate personal goals and influence the department's goals.

Mentor   An experienced professional who provides support to promote the development of new or less experienced persons.

Mentoring   The one-on-one sharing of practical, accumulated knowledge, often between a member of senior management to a person in training in the same department or organization.

Model   A person who serves as a target subject for a learner to emulate or a representation of a process or system that shows the most important variables in the system in such a way that analysis of the model leads to insights into the system.

Monitoring   An on-going process or system of reviewing a programme's activities through the collection of data and outputs to determine if set standards or requirements are being met.

Monitoring system   An on-going system to collect data on a programme's activities and outputs, designed to provide feedback on whether the programme is fulfilling its functions, addressing the targeted population and/or producing intended services.

Morale   The mental, emotional, and spiritual state of an individual.

Motivating   Using an individual's wants and needs to influence how the individual thinks and does. Motivating embodies using appropriate incentives and methods in reinforcing individuals or groups as they effectively work towards task accomplishment and resolution of conflicts or disagreements. Coupled with influence, motivating actively involves empowering junior leaders and workers to achieve organizational goals and properly rewarding their efforts as they achieve the goals.

Motivation   The combination of a person's desire and energy directed at achieving a goal. It is the cause of action.

Network   Individuals or organizations who share information, ideas, resources, or goals to accomplish individual or group goals.

Organization   A group of people identified by shared interests or purpose, for example, a business or the coordinating of separate elements into a unit or structure, the relationships that exist between separate elements arranged into a coherent whole, or efficiency in the way separate elements are arranged into a coherent whole.

Participative leadership   A leadership style in which the leader involves one or more employees in determining what to do and how to do it. The leader maintains final decision-making authority.

Partnership   A partnership is a business association of two or more people who have formally agreed to work together, each contributing skills, labour, and resources to the venture in return for an agreed share of the profits.

Professional   The term refers to members of those professions having a recognized status based upon acquiring professional knowledge through prolonged study. Examples of such professions include accountancy, actuarial computation, architecture, dentistry, engineering, law, medicine, nursing, pharmacy, and the sciences (e.g. biology, chemistry, physics, and teaching). To be a professional, a person must not only be qualified but also be involved in discharging corresponding professional duties.

Project   An undertaking with a specific objective and outcome that is to be met within a prescribed time cost and quality limitation.

Respect   Respect is treating people as they should be treated. Specifically, respect is indicative of compassion and consideration of others, which includes a sensitivity to and regard for the feelings and needs of others and an awareness of the effect of one's own behaviour on them. Respect also involves the notion of treating people justly.

Risk assessment   A method of analysing what risks exists, how likely they are to happen, and what the consequences would be.

Risk management   A general term describing the process of analysing risk in all aspects of management and operations and the development of strategies to reduce the exposure to such risks.

Skills (and competencies)   Those abilities that people develop and use with people, ideas, and things, hence, the division of interpersonal, cognitive, and technical skills.

Stakeholder   One who has a stake or interest in the outcome of the project.

Stakeholder expectations   Those products, functionality, benefits, etc. resulting from the project that stakeholders look forward to with some degree of certainty, rightly or wrongly. Discrepancies between stakeholder needs, specified requirements, expectations, and actual results can be a significant source of dissatisfaction with final project results.

Trait   A quality or characteristic of a person. For a trait to be developed in a person, the person must first believe in and value that trait.

Transactional leaders   Leaders who guide or motivate their followers in the direction of established goals by clarifying role and task requirements.

Trust   Belief in the integrity, character, and ability of a leader.

Values   The accepted principles or standards of an individual or a group or ideas about the worth or importance of things, concepts, and people.

Whistleblower   A person who expresses concern about possible malpractices or ethical issues.

Index

Page numbers followed by *t* and *f* indicates tables and figures, respectively.